1981

THE *MANAGERS*

CAREER ALTERNATIVES FOR THE COLLEGE EDUCATED

THE AUTHOR

Richard J. Thain's career has spanned a variety of sectors. For the past 13 years, he has been with the Graduate School of Business of the University of Chicago, where he is serving currently as assistant dean, director of placement, and a member of the teaching faculty. Previously he was a newspaper reporter, soldier-editor, advertising agency executive, and marketing professor.

In each of these roles, he has been a student of the career and job scene as well as a prolific writer whose articles have appeared in a number of journals. Over the years, he has noted that there is a paucity of material that describes the world of managerial and administrative work. With this volume he attempts to fill this gap.

Price $4.95

THE *MANAGERS*

CAREER ALTERNATIVES FOR THE COLLEGE EDUCATED

By Richard J. Thain

THE COLLEGE PLACEMENT COUNCIL, INC.

To Jane

FOREWORD

FOR TWO DECADES, both in business and in academia, I have counseled people about jobs and the careers to which they lead. Many of these counselees have been students or recent graduates of colleges and universities, but I do deal also with those in mid-career who are still exploring alternatives. I have likewise mediated between these aspirants and countless employer representatives.

As students and graduates brace themselves for careers, I find the most difficult aspect of their adjustment is to understand what goes on in "the real world" well enough to make intelligent job choices. Too frequently they are flying blind.

It is all very well to tell them, for example, that a career in banking can be rewarding, but this does not answer for them such crucial questions as what is involved in taking an entry-level job in a bank. "What will I be doing from 9 to 5 Monday through Friday and year to year as I progress?" This book was written to try to answer such questions.

Career, placement, and recruitment counselors are constantly being asked if they can recommend a book that will describe the kinds of administrative and managerial jobs into which college-trained people are likely to go. To date there is no such volume and most of us can recommend only placement articles and pamphlets here and there.

Happily on many college campuses formal courses have been developed to help students in career planning and placement. They have exposed a great need for the kinds of information contained in this book. Until now, however, there has been little written material that is helpful.

To fill the gaps, I have been asked by the College Placement Council to put these pages together. The Council is the central national organization representing college and university placement officers as well as recruiters from private business, government, and other institutions.

This volume limits its concerns to jobs requiring a college education, an area that, according to the U.S. Department of Labor, covers one out of every four jobs in this country. It focuses on jobs and career pathways in the managerial, administrative, and entrepreneurial arts and sciences. Combined, they form the greatest source of employment for college-trained people.

It would be impossible to trace every career pathway or individual job category, and so the aim has been to discuss those major areas where the principal activities lie.

The book has zeroed in on the specifics of job functions, rather than on differences between employer categories. After all, the function of an accountant is much the same at General Motors, at Health, Education and Welfare, or at Columbia University. The term "business" is used to apply equally to private enterprise, government, or public enterprise, and to not-for-profit enterprises. All are businesses to be run by the kinds of people for whom this book has been written.

While recognizing that a person starting out in the world is wise to think in terms of a career over many years, the book emphasizes the content of jobs in early career, following the trite but true statement that a long journey begins with the first step. It is important to think in long-range terms, but equally necessary and more pressing to know what you will do tomorrow and the Wednesday following. The only way to completely comprehend a job is to experience it. But a good book, while not experience, can report on the collected, refined, and compressed experience of hundreds of people. This tries to be such a book.

As this volume grew, it rather naturally fell into three categories, each designed to provide college and university students and graduates some handle to help them better grasp reality. The form of the book itself and some of its chapters is designed to examine the job world in broad macrocosm. First come the questions of what management is and what a manager does. Next, the major functional categories into which managerial work falls are treated.

Inevitably, the next step is to turn to the microcosm, to the specific job categories, to descriptions of what working people do. In each case, attention is paid to the personal traits and the kinds of education that are either useful or essential in a given career line.

Over and above the author's description of these jobs, it made sense to interview people at work. And so the volume contains the verbatim reports of live interviews plus case studies written by practitioners. For reasons of objectivity, the anonymity of those interviewed has been respected.

Thanks are due to these people, countless others who have had a hand in shaping this volume, and most particularly to the staff and officers of College Placement Council and my patient colleagues on the Communications Committee of that organization.

I am grateful also to the Graduate School of Business of the University of Chicago for rendering my time flexible enough to write and research the work. And, finally, there is a debt to Constance Hunt, my patient and literate editorial assistant.

CONTENTS

Further Observations

CHAPTER 1

THE MANAGEMENT PROFESSIONS

"A great society is a society in which its men of business think greatly of their functions."   **Alfred North Whitehead.**

FOR SOME CENTURIES, the traditional professions have been held to be Law, Medicine, Academia, and the Church. More recently, such fields as Engineering and Public Accounting have sprung into being. Of the business-related occupations, accountancy with its national set of examinations leading to the "C.P.A." designation has regarded itself as the most professional.

Gradually, with the rise of popularity of schools of business and public administration, the concept of professional management has gained widespread acceptance. Because of the diversity in administrative roles, it is perhaps more useful to employ the plural and call them the management professions.

In the face of the increasing complexities of private, public, and institutional business, it would seem logical for its practitioners to regard themselves as professionals.

One of the principal elements a recruiter looks for in interviewing prospective employees is a professional personal stance. Do they have some well articulated idea of who they are? Do they have some idea of where they stand in the welter of occupations of the present day and in the stream of history? Prospective employers prefer candidates with a developed occupational stance.

On what is such a stance built? It is partially based on a view of the professions of management akin to the view which young lawyers or doctors would have of their professions. Who practices the management professions? The manager, administrator, the executive. All of these terms can be used interchangeably, but what are they?

I once witnessed a debate in which a business school student was pitted against a self-styled radical student. The latter charged that the business school student was representative of a "new elite of profit-mongers out to run the world."

1

His opponent countered with the following: "As to profit, I believe in honest profit as necessary incentive. As to elite, you too, my friend, as a student at this university, represent an educational elite. As to running the world, there you've got it quite wrong. The business or government manager can at best only claim to try to help keep the crazy old world running in the sense of keeping human society on the rails. And it's a tough job and often a dirty one, but it is a job that needs doing and is worth doing."

Not trying to run the world, but trying to keep the world running. This is indeed a good summary of the task of the business manager or the government administrator. It is a tough job—often a dirty one, if you will. Not always glamorous, frequently anonymous, a manager works long and hard hours to keep recalcitrant society and its stubborn inhabitants running smoothly, rather than whirling in chaos. In many ways, this is the most important set of jobs in existence. Fortunately such work is rewarding, both from financial and psychic points of view.

When you stop and think of it, managers have been, since the Industrial Revolution, the inheritors of the leaders of all ages—the kings, generals, tribunes, merchants—yet they lack some of the power and glory of earlier leaders. Leadership is a demanding role at best and especially so where one has to lead by persuasion and rationality, rather than by brute strength or hereditary right.

Those managers who are not ultimate decision-makers are supporters of decision-makers, furnishing the figures, data, and thought and planning on which the more overt leaders must base their actions.

Economists underline the special nature of that intangible resource called management. The private business manager organizes and coordinates all other resources to produce something people want, and thereby earns a profit. From Ford Motor Company to the pizza parlor on your block, some person or group of people is coordinating the resources to produce products or services which meet needs and will thus sell.

Managers have to inspire people who are hard to inspire, and over whom they have no direct command, make decisions that are difficult choices. They have to shoulder responsibilities, work when they'd rather go to bed, raise money, sell ideas or products under difficult circumstances, open strange doors, meet payrolls, be a parent, mentor, teacher, disciplinarian. By and large, most managers carry work home with them in their briefcases or their heads. They can seldom drop their tools.

But then, somebody has to try to keep the human world running. It does not run well by itself.

CHAPTER 2

PREPPING FOR THE MANAGEMENT PROFESSIONS

ONE OF THE CHARACTERISTICS of a modern day profession is that it carries with it some formal educational requirements. The more traditional areas have required specific degrees, such as J.D. and M.D., plus passage of certain professional examinations. The management professions are somewhat less specific as to degrees and certification, though there is a tendency toward firming up such requirements.

Most of the professional-level jobs in larger businesses or government do call for at least a bachelor's degree. Such a base assumes an ability to read and write well, to figure adequately, and to possess enough familiarity with history, art, and science to fill a sensitive role within society.

Enough quantitative sophistication is demanded to comprehend the computer and the cybernetic techniques which lie behind the storage and retrieval of data so essential to modern management method.

Business management is inevitably a social scientific occupation. The business manager can be regarded as an applied social scientist in very much the same way as an engineer can be termed an applied scientist.

It is up to the manager to marshal the principles of economics in a way which effectuates the role of the organization. Managers are helped by a grasp of psychology in understanding what makes the human being tick. Such understanding is essential in motivating individuals to work creatively and effectively, to buy or sell, to vote or act.

Likewise, some understanding of political processes (political science) and of social processes (sociology) is desirable.

Generally this sophistication is advanced by a college education, culminating in a first degree, though we have all known non-degreed people who have picked up the requisites and been successful.

One of the saving characteristics of free and private enterprise is

4

that it has permitted people of all backgrounds to found and carry on successful businesses. In truth, ways have not been found to formally teach enterprise or daring or thrift or diligence very effectively.

The relatively uneducated business executive of the past grew up in an era when most people were comparatively unlettered and the executive was better informed than many contemporaries. Today, however, the number of non-degreed people rising in corporate enterprise is decreasing. Public enterprise is even stickier about degrees.

In a way that is not altogether desirable, we have aped military society in that a matter of a college degree separates the officer caste from the enlisted men and women, reserving the better job starts for the college educated and leaving the other jobs to clerical and "blue collar" people. Our society must plead guilty to imposing barriers against those who are not college educated.

All of this has become more complicated in recent years. Economic difficulties and occupational imbalances have created a sizable group of degreed people for whom no "suitable" work has been found. This has had two effects—the one to render a single degree (B.A. or B.S.) not enough, and the other to establish a whole category of what one multi-degreed student called "people of excess education." This is a harsh term for those with advanced degrees in non-marketable fields. For the most part, however, collegiate education in business skills at all levels has remained marketable through the good years and the lean years.

There is, of course, much more to education than sheer marketability, including education for creatively enjoying living and culture and leisure and one's companions. An old Scots proverb runs, "One becomes a philosopher or perishes." In the intellectual and spiritual sense, one may well perish who has not been educated to share in the stream of human experience that makes life at once richer and more bearable.

Be that as it may, there is the practical and occupationally related aspect to formal education. On this score, how can aspirants for careers in the management professions direct their educational investment?

First off, a well-rounded education culminating in a degree seems a minimal requirement. Like it or not, we do live in a degree-oriented society. Next, some attention to the keystone administrative subjects is called for.

Accounting is clearly a keystone. At many liberal arts colleges, a course or two in accounting can be taken and should be taken by the student who has no intention of graduate schooling in management. Math through calculus seems advisable as does some exposure to economics. Courses in marketing or management or finance may well be taken where possible as adjuncts to the B.A. degree.

Others may choose to major in business as undergraduates, devoting a sizable portion of the final two collegiate years to business subjects. This is a matter of election, since some business employers claim to be just as happy with the Bachelor of Arts (particularly with the addition of a few business courses) as with a Bachelor of Science in Business Administration.

For those intending to go on to graduate work in business or public administration, the undergraduate major in business is regarded as redundant by many graduate schools. They tend to prefer the broader background which the arts and sciences provide.[1]

Engineering in most of its forms can be a good backdrop for business. In the more technical industrial areas, an engineering or other technical undergraduate background (i.e., computer science, math, physics, chemistry) may be required. More engineers may wind up in business and administration than in engineering. The same may hold true for law graduates, and law also can be said to provide a good graduate background for business.

As with most professions, the more professional education of quality one has, the better off one is. "The future belongs to those who prepare for it" is a reality as well as a slogan.

What of the Master of Business Administration, Master of Public Administration, and related degrees?[2] Such additional one to two years of professional school are increasingly the ticket for good entry-level jobs.

---

[1] For a discussion of graduate business schools and their entry requirements, see the pamphlet "Prepping for a Profession," by Richard J. Thain, available through many college placement offices or from the College Placement Council, Inc., P.O. Box 2263, Bethlehem, Pa. 18001.

[2] Some equivalents to the more common Master of Business Administration degree are the Master of Science in Industrial Administration and Master of Management. Master of Science in Accountancy is typical of a more specialized advanced degree. The Master of Public Administration is self-explanatory, although in some schools it becomes an M.B.A. with a public administration major, concentration, or specialty. The

Graduate business schooling does not necessarily require previous academic work in administration or management, and, as noted already, some schools actually frown upon undergraduate business majors. Quite a few graduate institutions do favor full-time work experience before application, though others are just as happy with newly minted B.A. or B.S. graduates.

Is the M.B.A. essential? As will be pointed out in the following pages, for some of the fields such as management consulting and brand management, an M.B.A. degree is a virtual requirement. As we move through descriptions of the major management occupations, the normal degree requirements for these sectors will be noted.

Just as does the Bachelor of Business degree, the Master's degree covers the major functional areas (i.e., accounting, marketing, finance), but covers them at a higher and more intensive level. The increasing popularity of the business degrees at both levels is testimony to their market value. American employers are usually hard-headed people who do not fancy paying out extra money for empty strings of degrees.

Once upon a time, a Master's degree was a rarity, almost a frill. Clarence Randall, the late chairman of Inland Steel Company, was fond of telling how he had to hide two college degrees in order to get a start in the steel business 60 years ago. College attendees were regarded as too effete to survive in the steel business. Now, with increasing numbers of proven executives holding them, graduate degrees have become standards of entry into a number of the management occupations in the steel and many other industries.

Still, cautions must be issued about graduate work and any tendency to prolong schooling and collect degrees for their own sakes. Graduate business schools are now partially peopled with advanced-degree-holders from other disciplines. It can be difficult for an older student equipped with an M.A. or a Ph.D. in the humanities to establish believability as a potential business administrator—even with the addition of a fresh M.B.A. degree. We are still prisoners of the experience tracks we have laid behind us and must convince employers

same is true of Master of Hospital Administration, which is often offered as an M.B.A. Ph.D. degrees in Business, Management, or Public Administration or the Doctor of Business Administration are the common highest degrees in the field, although the M.B.A. is regarded as "terminal" equipment for most managerial jobs and doctoral graduates tend to go into teaching and research.

that we are prepared both educationally and emotionally to set off in new directions.

There are, in the eyes of employers, such things as having too much education (in an inappropriate area). With every year of age, it becomes more difficult to start over again.

The problems of postponing career entry by extending collegiate study can be avoided by night-time or part-time schooling after one is launched in a private or public business career. In many cities, there are some part-time business programs offered at all levels for administrators and would-be administrators to attend while on a full-time job.

Such programs are popular with degree-holding professionals from other fields, such as science, law, medicine, education, the church, the military. These people all have one thing in common: they have taken or are about to take managerial posts (i.e., as medical administrators, church officials, research directors, etc.). These posts demand that they use another set of mental muscles than did their original callings. They must manage people and budgets, hire, fire, and meet payrolls. There is no better proof that the management professions stand on their own bottoms as separate disciplines than the recognition accorded them by these retooling members of other professions.

CHAPTER 3

ASSESSING PERSONAL TRAITS

EVERY YEAR I run into cases of graduating students who fail to get the job they want. Oh, they get a job all right, but the most prized alternative somehow eludes them. It is not necessarily a case of those with less than spectacular academic records. Often the opposite is true. Here is an actual case in point.

Willard B. sits before me, at once crestfallen and irate. "Will you tell me," he implores, "why my roommate with a 2.8 academic average got the job I wanted? My grade point is 3.7, and I test much higher than he does too. Where is the justice?" He casts his eyes heavenward as if to accuse God after the fashion of Tevya, the central character in "Fiddler on the Roof."

The roommate is a person of more charm, vigor, presence, assertiveness, enthusiasm, and professional perspective than the man who sits before me. Of course, I cannot be blunt and tell him all of these things. As a counselor, I must employ indirection and say, "Well, think about what your friend has that you do not."

Upon reflection, my visitor begins to perceive what previously he either did not or would not perceive about management jobs. Many such jobs are more dependent upon the suitability of personal traits than upon such elements as grades and test scores. In this way, they may differ markedly from jobs in some of the established professions such as law, where most of the "best" jobs tend to go to the academic leaders of the class.

It would be foolish to deny that grades in college or graduate work do not weigh in hiring decisions. When in doubt, earn the higher grade. Attention to grades varies from employer to employer and industry to industry. Management consultants demand very high grades in graduate work. Public accounting firms want good grades. Some of the employers in the marketing area pay less attention to grades, particularly in personal selling. This does not mean that the less grade conscious professions are more lax or less demanding. It merely emphasizes that there is less connection between academic performance and the kinds of intelligence and skill demanded.

Employers pay considerable attention to work experience. For younger applicants, this will of necessity be of a part-time and school vacation variety.

At a recent meeting of recruiters from industry, who make a career of interviewing on college campuses, a consensus was reached. Some 67 people present agreed that their interviews hinge upon two kinds of factors. The first set includes the "here and now," that is, how impressed is the recruiter with the actions, personality, and appearance of the candidate? The second set is comprised of past behavior. What is there in the past behavior of the person that predicts success on the job the company has to offer?

Recruiters will probe an interviewee's past, looking for successes and influences in school and work history that predict future success. Thus, it is wise for interviewees to refine in their own minds those past experiences and accomplishments which point to future business accomplishment.

Extracurricular activities in school are likewise important to an employer. Students must weigh how much time they can spend on outside employment or activities and still keep their grades up.

There also is a cosmetic element to managerial hiring, part of the "here and now." This is not to say that one must be handsome or beautiful, but certainly it helps to be an attractive person. Some of the external traits can be telling in close decisions. Personal effectiveness and carriage and even grooming will count, given two applicants of similar educational achievement.

Most managerial jobs call for personal effectiveness, although they do vary a great deal in the extent to which working with other people is an important feature of the job. Inherent shyness or inwardness is the greatest single enemy to effectiveness in the managerial professions. In almost all such jobs, staff or line, one must be able to sell ideas, to persuade, to communicate, yes, and at times, cajole and coerce people into doing what initially they may be opposed to doing.

In the areas we are discussing, every man, every woman is a sales person, selling his or her ideas and personal values to a wide range of other people, all of them customers.

While it is hard to generalize about traits which lead to success in the employment process and later on the job, it can be said that the management professions do call for a certain level of assertiveness. This is not necessarily overtly aggressive behavior. Nevertheless, it is necessary for successful practitioners to state their ideas and positions politely, but firmly. As one industry recruiter put it, "Our company is no place for little gray mice. Our big tiger cats will eat them alive."

Other factors which managerial candidates must consider are the traits of employers. Every company has a history and a personality that reflects the people which make it up, with heavier influences coming from those at the top. Some people are acquired by companies into which they never really fit. One young woman, talking about her company, said, "I was placed in a sort of 'coventry,' that is, the other people in my section did not invite me to socialize with them or to lunch with them. Oh, they were polite enough and accepted my work, but we were of different backgrounds. I didn't care for them either. I regard myself as an urban type, and I thought they were 'preppie' suburbanites. Eventually I felt I had to go elsewhere, even though I rather liked the work."

And another person, angling for an educational administration job, said, "Universities are rather clubby places. I knew I had won the job when, as I was leaving the dean's office, I overheard him saying to his associates, 'Well, at least we've found a person who has a chance of being one of us.' The ability to be one of them was more important than any other qualification I possessed."

This fit or feel or ambience can be geographic, or educational, or a matter of social class. We Americans sometimes pretend that in our society there is no social classhood, but it exists, though perhaps in somewhat less overt forms than in some of the other nations.

For example, a public accountant once admitted that his firm did not hire Ivy League graduates because the firm felt they had a tendency not to mix well socially with their peers from the giant Midwestern state universities who comprised the bulk of the staff. "They move in different circles, you know," was his comment.

One can consult any of various sociology texts and possibly determine where one falls insofar as social class and taste are concerned, but a certain feel of rapport or lack of it is probably the surest judge in such matters.

A job aspirant should talk to as many potential peers and superiors within the hiring organization as possible before joining. Just knowing the recruiters, who never may be seen again, is scarcely enough. The crucial questions to ask about an organization are: "What are the people like who work there now? What kinds of people have done well there and have reached the top? How much like them am I?"

Of course, one of the helpful facts about human beings is that they are subject to change. Every place exerts a subtle socialization pressure, often subconscious, upon the people who work there. Gradually, imperceptibly, most folks working there modify their attitudes, habits, and social traits to conform to the norms of the institution.

The dangers of inbreeding are obvious. Likes tend to hire likes. That's why some organizations work hard to hire some people from outside the wall, rather than just to promote from within. That's why some employers make conscious efforts to hire from a variety of different schools and regions. They want to avoid incestuousness. But it's tough to be different, and we all have to judge for ourselves how much of a pioneer we want to be by going with an institution where we stand out as a variant of the norm.

By the time a young person is part way through the college years, the individual should have some idea of strengths and weaknesses. Do I write well? Am I analytical? Do people react favorably to me? Am I overly shy, overly pushy? Negative traits can be viewed simply as an inventory of givens or can be seen as weaknesses to be overcome, to be altered, to be worked on. Some, but not all such characteristics are amenable to alteration.

Self-assessment is the start for any career planning exercise, and it is rendered difficult because of the problem one has in seeing oneself objectively. But the attempt should be made with the help of self, friends, and placement-career counselors.

College or university career counseling and placement offices are for the most part eager and able to help. Most are chronically understaffed, however, and a student must display the desirable trait of persistence to get an appointment. Counselors can provide a trained and objective point of view, and can be confidantes of maturity and wisdom. Youth matures by experience, but also by interfaces with older people.

Placement counselors can direct the younger person to various kinds of tests that can be a helpful complement to self-assessment or face-to-face assessment by a counselor. There are tests for aptitudes or potentials for acquiring specific types of knowledge, such as computer programming skills. Then there are interest tests which cover the range of likes and dislikes and take stock of intelligence and non-intelligence skills, as well as determine what occupations one is suited for. Personality tests aiming for an insight into emotional make-up, stability, and adjustment make some sense, but total reliance on any test does not make sense.

For somewhat older career planners and seekers, alumni placement counselors can be helpful. Customarily, colleges and universities also provide some form of placement system that will match the experienced seeker to jobs.

There are a few outside career counseling firms that can be relied upon to help in personal evaluation through testing and introspection. Where they exist, local college placement offices will probably know who they are.

CHAPTER 4

CAREER PLANS AND PATHS

BEGINNING CAREERISTS should cast an eye toward the long-run nature of professional work. One reason why the initial job after college or university is so important is that it sets the graduate out in a direction which, though not necessarily final, will be increasingly harder to change every year thereafter. In theory, it is nice to contemplate a life in which one changes jobs as easily as clothes, a life which can become a rich wardrobe of varied experiences. In practice, it is hard to move from one kind of work to another. Employers are habitually slot-minded. They tend to want people for jobs who have performed the same role before. Society at times seems bent on punishing those who seek variety.

There are certain kinds of occupational changes that are regarded as logical, however. It is common for public accounting auditors to move into corporate accounting or financial jobs, or for bank commercial lending officers to move into corporation treasury work. These "bounce-offs" are considered logical because the kinds of jobs involved are closely related. Even so, the tide seldom flows the other way. Accounting firms and banks are noted for the training they provide, and the flow runs outward from the schooling site.

Actually what matters very greatly in career pathways is an advancement related to previous work or to newly completed education. Employers admire planners whose resumes show congruent progression and are skeptical of those whose careers wander all over the spectrum.

The job market has a tendency to allow only so many changes of employment. This varies according to industry. People in the advertising agency business are likely to be permitted more employer switches than are bankers, for example.

Changing jobs just for the sake of change or a little extra salary is ill-advised. Too many changes mark a person as an unreliable "job hopper." One can find successful careers where the hero has been a restless gun. But you look around and find another equally successful man or woman who has been with one employer for a whole career.

Still, a change in work is often what is needed to stimulate a dull life. The switcher may have been trapped underneath an unsympathetic or unappreciative boss. He may have come to be viewed as "just old George," when he regards himself as a new George with new skills and new training and an urge to "get off the dime."

It is important for each man or woman to retain a sense of verve and romance about a career. The most successful people by their own judgments, and, after all, isn't that what really counts, are those who have a sense of their own worth and a sense of drama about themselves. They are the lead characters in their own plays and are excited about their parts. An ability to transmit such excitement ranks along with competence as an important element in attracting other people to them.

By switching to another department or another employer, one may be able to renew zest for work and become a fresh new face to a cast of new bosses and subordinates.

Such moves are not without their toll. In transferring employers, one may make a premature move and miss out on some favorable plans which the previous employer had in mind. It is always wise to "check back at the ranch" to find out as best you can what the plans are for you before diving headlong into a new job with a new organization, leaving behind familiarity, continuity, old loyalties, and more tangible assets such as pensions and benefits. Giving the old place a first chance to bid for your services against new opportunities can make good sense.

Man has been called "the planning animal" by anthropologists. Most professional managers eventually are accorded a strong hand in planning the future of their organizations. Yet, comparatively few professional managers have attempted to plan their own careers. "Attempted" is the key word, since there are so many external, uncontrollable factors involved as to render it unlikely that plans will succeed in all respects. The important thing is that a plan be set down and adjusted periodically to match changing conditions.

Career path determination by the individual naturally starts with self-assessment, together with plans for exploiting strong points or strengthening weak ones. All elements should be committed to paper from the outset.

Next a series of advancements within the present organization or other organizations should be plotted. It is vital to assign some tentative dates, since careers have an inevitable way of slipping by swiftly.

Personal planning is necessary because one cannot usually count upon superiors or organizations to do much planning for individuals. Oh, they pay lip service to it and talk about management development and organization development, but too often it does not go much farther than talk.

If lucky, one may find oneself with an organization which cooperates with employees in allowing them at least a hand in planning their own programs. With similar fortune, a graduate may work for a boss who will talk career with subordinates. Theoretically, every superior should be concerned with developing subordinates as successors. But many bosses find this difficult to perform, because they find it painful to think of being succeeded by anyone. Subordinates typically find their bosses much too busy with day-to-day affairs to talk to them about occupational plans.

Lacking external support for career planning, too many managerial hopefuls find their futures encased in mysterious black boxes. The only way they can find keys is to forge their own by thinking carefully about their moves and attempting to unlock or force open the box.

Young people usually have to keep doggedly reminding their superiors of their plans, of their restlessness, of their availability, of their skills and values. Of course, all this presupposes strong performance and demonstrated value. Good work is the ultimate leverage on the black box.

To a young person whose career stretches out ahead for 45 years, time may seem an inconsequential factor, but this is an illusion. Despite governmental strictures against discrimination in hiring on the basis of age, anyone who is older than 40 or in a position to observe the employment scene knows that our rather youth-oriented society is quite discriminatory, quite "agist" in its attitudes. We have probably moved further in erasing sex barriers than age barriers.

In the military occupations there is a term "overage in grade" which describes the person who is too old for the rank held and is non-promotable. Such a situation leads to dismissal or early retirement.

Civilian economic sociology offers some parallels. We have already talked about the officer (college graduate) caste vs. the enlisted (non-college white and blue collar) categories. Likewise, in many a corporation or financial institution or government bureau, there are clearly demarcated ranks through which one moves upward in a career, armed with such outward show as larger offices, pay, and perquisites, even though stars and bars are not worn on the shoulders.

Likewise, we live in an employment atmosphere where hiring is done in terms of age milestones. We tend to think in terms of five-year ranges—of people, say, 20 to 25, 25 to 30, 30 to 35, 35 to 40, etc.

As people approach the upper limits of these ranges, they may become worried and restless. For example, in our alumni placement office at the Graduate School of Business, University of Chicago, we notice a considerable bulge of applicants for placement help at ages 29 and 30, 34 and 35, and 38 and 39. Magic markers of 30, 35, and 40 tend to drive achievers of these ages into our office to count the candles and to plot strategies for faster progress.

What is more significant, perhaps, is that employers view these age markers as real barriers, though these days they do not enunciate these attitudes publicly.

CHAPTER 5

TIMETABLES FOR COLLEGE GRADUATES

SINCE WE SEEM to be dealing with a system which dances to a five-year meter, it could be wise to take this rhythm into account in life planning. It should be possible to develop a rough but useful description of a career timetable for a promising young college graduate in private or public business. This is set up here for a B.A. or B.S.-degree-holder. Graduate work will postpone the start, but there is evidence that graduate-degree-holders will quickly catch up and in many cases eclipse their lower-degreed competitors.

CAREER TIMETABLE FOR
FOUR-YEAR COLLEGE GRADUATES
Ages 20 to 25

This is the training and orientation period during which the newcomer earns his or her spurs. Leaving an employer during this period may cut short the practical training experience before full benefit is had out of it. Frequently the neophyte learns an initial specialty. Most of what a person has to sell at this point is potential and promise.

Ages 25 to 30

The maturing aspirant enters the perfection of specialty phase during which the individual can claim some expertise in a functional area and come to learn the organization, its people, its products, or services, its market environment. First supervisory experience is usually gained at this level. The careerist is no longer a trainee and has a proven record and set of skills to sell.

Ages 30 to 35

First heavy responsibilities crop up. At this point, a "staff" functionary becomes a senior in charge of other specialists, teams, and

18

projects. People in line jobs gain substantial command roles. People engaged in support work who are going to make it into command and decision posts usually make their jump from staff to line in these years. There are always exceptions, but it tends to be at this point that the climbers have the feel that they have found the trail for the remainder of the ascent and begin to have first intimations of really just how far they will go.

Ages 35 to 40

So-called "fast track" people may move into general management. General management comprises those positions which transcend specialty and place a person in charge of more than one functional area (i.e., a previous factory production manager takes additional charge of all sales and financial activity of a plant). This leap upward is crucial for those who will become high officers of an organization. Public accountants and consultants become partners (or equivalents) either here or in the brackets just above or below this.

Ages 40 to 45

Staff or support people rise to head their specialties (for example, a researcher becomes director of research and development). Command managers come into their own as vice presidents or presidents or directors of a broad section of activities within an organization. But not all people are on such fast tracks. Many find the level here beyond which they may never move. They "plateau out," as business jargon has it.

Ages 45 to 50

In large organizations, this may still be the leaping point into general management or higher officership. In such seniority-oriented organizations, it may take time to rise. Middle-level managers may not rise to full potential in such organizations until this period.

Ages 50 to 55

Most executives have hit their final level, but some are moving into high jobs in their own or other organizations. Movement outside one's own company is largely restricted to the loftier jobs at these ages. Most others are becoming too old in grade for movement.

Ages 55 to 65

Some movement, but largely a period of consolidation. In some companies, retirement is mandatory or duties are decreased. In certain institutions such as universities, administrative academics must return to being academics. Once again, there are always exceptions and individual cases of late blooming.

One great argument for continual stock taking, even for keeping a set of written career predictions and objectives in a drawer, and checking and revising them from time to time, is that one will be alert to and reactive to a changing scenario. While we are not exactly captains of our fate, we may play pilot or first mate.

Those who are sensitive to the nuances of movement about them will by say age 35 have some idea of whether or not they are going to reach their maximum ambitions. Various signals are provided through promotions, reviews, perquisites, and relationships with higher officials.

There are three ways to react to such intimations. The first, which should always be exerted, is to attempt to gain a hearing from superiors to propose new directions, to protest progress blocks, shuntings, and grievances. In a surprising number of cases, such action works.

A second alternative is to attempt to move to another organization. Thirdly, there is adaption and rationalization. This is where the careerist says, "I'll settle for what I have and do the best job I can to be strong in my own sphere, limited though it may be." Such an attitude brings with it answers to the urge of competence and the urge for self-respect.

People who have settled for what they are today may enrich their lives in professional improvement. Numerous people who have derived great satisfaction for themselves in politics, charitable enterprises, education, hobbies, sports, have carried on these activities simultaneously with a full-time job where they know they have peaked. Often they can devote the requisite time and energy to projects which benefit not just themselves, but others.

There are many ways to the success that counts, which is a state of satisfaction with life. Not all people feel the "divine discontent" which may motivate those who scale the peaks. Climbing foothills to sunny plateaus has its attractions.

While occupational satisfaction is an important ingredient in life, it is certainly not the only ingredient. Meaningful work is important to most people, but it usually needs to be balanced with other pursuits and preoccupations. The so-called "workaholic" can be both sick and frustrated. Likewise, the person who expects the company to minister completely to the individual's creative needs will probably wind up disenchanted by these over-expectations.

Others who may suffer from disenchantment are the increasing numbers of college and university students at older ages. They are coming back to school, full or part-time, at ages high enough to throw the timetables described earlier in this chapter into comparative uselessness for the people in question. For further exploration of this subject, please see the later chapter, entitled "Special Opportunities and Problems for Older Students and Graduates."

CHAPTER 6

LINE AND STAFF

ALLUSIONS ARE MADE in the timetable offered in the previous chapter to "line" and "staff" career paths. These terms are part of the parlance of business, government, and the military, taking their origins from the latter.

The armies of history have long made distinctions between line officers and staff officers. The former have traditionally had direct command over fighting troops; the latter have headed groups which support those troops by acting as planning advisors or by heading such support functions as supply (quartermaster), transportation, medicine, food, and recreation.

Applied to civilian pursuits, the distinctions have become blurred by the complexity of such realms, but they do exist in the minds of practitioners and are hence important.

Certain functions are traditionally regarded as line. Principal among these are top officer posts: chairpersons, presidents, and various levels of vice presidents who occupy general management posts. They have their government equivalents in chief executives and department directors, and in colleges, in presidents and deans.

Such top administrators are in command of subordinates. They have the ultimate power to hire and fire, though such power may be hedged these days by various review processes.

It is the ultimate duty of these top line officials to make decisions and to issue commands to their subordinates for implementation of these decisions.

These subordinates may be line or staff. Line subordinates execute the commands of their superiors, much the way that a captain of a company of soldiers leads his men into battle on command of a line superior, the colonel of his regiment. The colonel, in turn, is passing down through channels the orders of a general of the brigade, who received his orders from a corps commander, who, in turn, is responsible to a supreme commander.

The commanding general at the top is also advised by a general staff of high ranking experts who do not command troops. They marshal not men, but ideas, plans, logistics, tactics, figures.

Thus, the line organization of a company presents similar kinds of officials. The chief executive officer (C.E.O.) is armed with planners, people whose duty it is to furnish the data and ideas upon which to make decisions. These staff people have no command powers, except over their own subordinates, and make no direct decisions, though, of course, they have some power over what to present or withhold from the chief.

Lower line officials derive their powers from their direct bosses. Someone in charge of a manufacturing plant may be nearly autonomous in power over those who work at the plant and make a host of smaller "life and death" decisions in a day.

The staff chief, on the other hand, may have hiring and firing rights over subalterns, but not fiat to make other decisions which alter the course of company policy. Staff people operate in an advisory capacity and line people in an implementive capacity, with a mandate both to issue orders of their own and carry out orders from the top.

Among the traditional line functions in business have been those of marketing, particularly the sub-function of sales. Carrying out the military analogy, sales people are front-line soldiers in a sales campaign.

Right behind them are some other line people such as the workers on the assembly line, their supervisors, and their plant manager. They furnish the ammunition, so to speak.

A line sales manager may have staffers—marketing people and sales support assistants. Likewise, the production manager is backed by a staff of industrial engineers, timekeepers, and personnel people.

And, as we will see, many people considered to be "on the line," such as brand managers of packaged goods companies, have little direct command over all the people they must coordinate, such as advertising agency people, sales managers, and production managers.

And the top financial executives of a company, though they may be called "staff," are so close to the mainstream of the life of the company's major decisions that they can scarcely be counted as purely advisory, purely staff. One hears of line financial officers and staff financial officers.

The old distinctions between line and staff may be coalescing in the complex modern organization with its great emphasis upon planning and information systems. Staff people are now very close to the running of the company, vital to its decisions and to their implementation.

We have spoken some and will speak more about personal equipment valuable to business leaders. Such traits as assertiveness and command charisma are more important to line executives than to staff. A shy person may indeed be suitable as a technical planner or information specialist.

It is important for future managers to think of whether their likes and instincts and personal characteristics are best adapted to command or to advisory functions and to plot a course accordingly.

It can be perceived that many a career will embrace both line and staff work. Young planners advising a top line officer may catch the fancy of the boss and be placed ultimately in their own command. Zigs and zags in and out of line and staff positions are common.

Many well educated beginners, such as M.B.A.'s, start in a staff specialty. Their schooling has endowed them with a knowledge of financial theory, of accounting, of computers that naturally causes them to be employed as near experts from the start.

After a few years, if one has line ambitions, the real trick will be to vault above one's specialty into a command post that includes other specialties within one's span of control.

Specialties are initially valuable to a careerist who would start out as more than a green trainee. But those who have such a specialty can be imprisoned in a comfortable trap out of which they probably must be sprung somewhere in their 30s or consign themselves to being staff officials for the rest of their days. Of course, there are worse fates.

CHAPTER 7

BUSINESS FIELDS OPEN
TO COLLEGE GRADUATES

THE WORLD of employment appears baffling because people are involved in so many different jobs. Actually, upon closer examination, these jobs fall into a comparatively small number of fairly distinct categories in one of three settings: private business, non-profit institutions, or government.

The major functional categories include: **marketing,** which covers sales, advertising, purchasing, merchandising, and physical distribution of goods, including transportation, warehousing, and storage. People who market or move or sell or promote tangible goods, such as food, clothing, toothpaste, or automobiles, are obviously in different sorts of industries than those who market services, including such intangible wares as money loans, repair services, vacations, political candidates, religion, ideas.

While we are not in the habit of thinking of government bureaus and universities as selling or marketing institutions, the government spends millions to sell its citizens on such ideas as fuel conservation. A university is selling its services to new students (admissions), its graduates to employers (placement), and its financial supporters such as foundations, governments, and wealthy individuals (development).

Those companies which sell goods to other businesses, for example, machinery to factories or floor cleaning fluid to office building managers, are usually said to be in industrial marketing or marketing to the trade.

Those companies selling to the so-called "ultimate" consumers, individuals and households, are generally characterized as engaged in consumer marketing.

Later chapters will describe the key jobs in marketing, including such specialties as advertising agencies and retailing. Each of the other functional areas will be examined in similar detail.

Accounting jobs are everywhere. Almost every conceivable type of human organization keeps a set of books, not that there isn't more to collegiate-level accounting work than sheer bookkeeping. Accountants must set up systems and organize figures into statements of what a company owns, owes, has done, and ought to do in the future.

Though there is a tendency to think of accountants in terms of "C.P.A.'s," as public accountants are popularly known, the majority of accountants do not hold the C.P.A. designation and are engaged in what is known as industrial accounting, or management accounting, or private accounting. They work directly for corporations, governments, or institutions, rather than for the independent consultative firms in which public accountants band together.

Frequently industrial accountants bear job titles such as financial analyst, auditor, systems analyst, credit analyst. As such, they may be confused by outside observers with knowledge workers in the financial or data processing areas. The closeness with which the job is allied with the control (controllership or comptrollership) functions should determine whether the job lies in accounting or finance, or both.

Finance. No matter where you put the accent in this common functional word, it covers a multitude of jobs. Many of them call for M.B.A. training, and this is an area where graduate school of business professors have concentrated much of their advanced, cutting-edge research.

A common introductory job in finance with a corporation is that of a financial analyst. The basic activity is monitoring the needs for and the uses of money and other assets within the corporation or institution.

Financial analytic positions, a strong staple for M.B.A. and some B.S. and B.A. graduates, may lie close to the accounting side of the company or over to the treasury side, the latter having to do with the corporation's employment and investment of its own funds. There is considerable variety in the functions from employer to employer.

Under the broad blanket of financial jobs, we will consider the lending, saving, and money facilitating activities carried on by the commercial banks, savings and loan associations, and credit unions. We will likewise take a look at jobs in investment banking and brokerage firms which have to do with buying and selling various stocks and bonds which industries and governments float to raise financial capital for themselves.

A number of college graduates are employed by insurance companies, investment advisory firms, and mutual funds as managers of the funds invested through various arrangements (portfolios).

Investment and sales jobs alike are open from time to time in real estate. Insurance jobs are usually very available alternatives.

It has been noted that a number of the jobs in finance are reserved for holders of advanced degrees. Accounting, while leaning toward advanced degrees, still employs the majority of its beginners out of undergraduate schools, usually, but not exclusively, those with accounting majors.

Banks and other financial institutions continue to draw some of their people from the ranks of bachelor's-degree holders, though they draw substantially from graduate business schools also.

Data Processing or Information Systems activity is closely tied in with every other phase of management. Financial, accounting, and marketing people are dependent upon the people who run computers and organize programs upon them. From computer programmer trainee on up through overall directors of data processing, there are various jobs for college graduates of all backgrounds.

Production or manufacturing lies on the technical side of management, as does computer work. These areas are likely to call for engineering schooling, although math and science majors, liberal arts and business undergrads, and M.B.A.'s are also hired. Production managers supervise the people who run the machines. Many of them are line commanders of the areas they supervise. They schedule production runs and deal with budgeting as well as employee relations. There also are staff support jobs which provide the line manager with the requisite information for decisions. Often the information is computer generated.

Production is one common way to break into what is somewhat confusingly called general management or **general administration**. The term "general management" is used to refer to the overall management at the top that presides over all functional areas. Trainee jobs rather broadly conceived may be better described as generally administrative. The young person starts off in a minor management role for training and may then be rotated through a variety of functions and locations, perhaps spending a career of great diversity which, if not too unfocused, can be good preparation for later, higher management roles.

Individual companies and industries vary a great deal in the length and comprehensiveness of their training programs. Banks and accounting firms are strong on training, as are some brand management firms.

Graduates likewise differ in their reactions toward training. Some regard it as an important extension of school. Others, particularly older graduates with advanced degrees, feel they have had enough education already.

Young job aspirants may be surprised to find that a functional category called simply "management" has not been listed. This surprise can be laid to the fact that many business schools have functional departments of management, just as they have departments of accounting, marketing, and finance. Actually, "management" refers to the whole spectrum of managerial jobs and not to any specific functional set.

General administration, often called **office administration**, could be used for a potpourri of managerial jobs which do not fit the other functional categories. People in these positions are keeping things running in miscellaneous ways. Specific training for such roles is naturally hard to come by and a miscellany of educational experiences may lead to them. As always, when in doubt, economics and the other social sciences and some business courses make a fitting cap to a good broad education.

Personnel or **human resources management** is that specialized portion of general administration charged with training, evaluating, hiring, and discharging personnel. Record keeping is part of this function. Increasingly counseling skills have become important along with advanced degree preparation.

Industrial relations is that section of personnel work identified with the relations between a company and its workers, often wage-hour workers. Negotiations between these workers, their unions, and their employers fall within this bailiwick. Legal training can be helpful for collegians going into this sector.

CHAPTER 8

THE PEOPLE PEOPLE

VARIOUS JOBS calling for college training lie in **Personnel**. Some people regard that word as an old fashioned one and use **Human Resources** to describe the functions. Simply stated, it is the job of personnel people to manage the systems that govern the relationship of the organization to the people who make it up.

Now that's a big order rendered a bit less ambitious by an axiom in administration that every superior is responsible for developing, helping, and supporting subordinates. If this actually worked out in practice, there would be less need for personnel people than there is. But there is some tendency on the part of bosses, superintendents, and supervisors to fulfill their part in the personnel compact quite unevenly. And that's where personnel comes in, to complement these efforts.

Personnel could be called a classic staff function. Such people do not directly command others (except their own assistants) and they seldom make decisions which directly involve the stance of the organization toward the outer world. For this reason, personnel people often consider themselves relatively powerless in the total life of the organization. Where this is true, it is surely regrettable. How could there be a more important set of functions than those affecting people? In the final analysis, buildings, machines, products are unimportant compared to the people who use them. This can be especially true in the growing proportion of service industries. Top executives of such companies as banks and public accounting firms are fond of saying, "Our inventory goes up and down the elevators every night."

The details of handling these human inventories fall to the personnel people. They recruit new employees and then help train them. They assist line bosses in evaluating performance, setting compensation, and in promoting and firing people. It is their job to help sustain morale, a sense of participation and well-being among all employees.

It is fairly obvious that jobs in the human resources area put stress on collegiate training in the behavioral or psychological area. Advanced degrees and some specialization can be desirable, both to provide background and to differentiate candidates for personnel jobs, but B.A. and B.S. graduates are often considered for such jobs. The demand for new and inexperienced graduates has not been strong for some years, but the demand for experienced people has been fairly good. The trick for the young is how to gain some experience. Willingness to start modestly may be the clue.

Law training can be useful in several corners of the people occupations, including a subset known as **Industrial Relations**, the area in and through which the company deals with its employees and with their representatives, the unions. Much that goes on here involves negotiations over labor contracts and employee grievances. Governmental and external refereeing bodies are often involved.

Another area aligned with law is compliance with governmental strictures regarding racial minorities and women. Whatever other effect such laws have had, they have unquestionably created jobs for large numbers of personnel people. The majority of human resources jobs, however, do not call specifically for legal training.

Statistical, mathematical, and actuarial schooling can be ingredients in the training mix for people interested in working on the various compensation problems involved in personnel activity. These revolve around the setting of pay scales and options for wage workers, white collar workers, and managerial employees. The latter are likely to be paid through complexes of arrangements, deferred and present, designed to provide attractive alternatives to straight salary, to offer access to ownership of companies, and to avoid or defer the payment of certain kinds of income taxes. In this category lie references to stock options, deferred compensation, and profit sharing.

Employees at all levels are covered by pension programs. Complex arrangements in this regard call for people with good quantitative backgrounds to work on them and with them.

There are strong elements of both teaching and counseling in jobs in the human resources area. Many personnel people are heavily involved in training both new hires and people who have been around for a while who need refresher training. Some of this is done in classroom settings, while quite a bit of it is performed on the job by immediate supervisors. Such jobs can quite naturally place stress on backgrounds in teaching, courses in education or in related counseling.

Counseling tends to be a species of one-on-one teaching. Empathetic people who "relate" well to others and are patient and sympathetic listeners inevitably make good personnel counselors who can hear fellow employees out on work-related problems and certain personal problems as well. Few employers can afford to offer complete personal and social counseling, but they are relied upon to provide some such service.

As is true of any of the species of jobs discussed to date, it would be ridiculous to characterize personnel management jobs as totally absorbing, interesting, or psychically rewarding. There is a lot of routine to be carried out, the checking of time cards, the processing of insurance claims, the enormous paper work incident to the filling out of forms and reports of the sort that today's society and government demand.

To a certain extent, the function of "ombudsman" is filled by personnel people. A pure ombudsman is an advocate for the employee, a person who will stick up for the employee's rights and will intercede with the employer where there seems to be just cause to do so; in short, a listener and a champion. Of course, ombudsmen are usually employed by management, except in rare cases where they are union-management joint employees. It is an interesting concept and a rare sort of job to get. In most cases, the people people settle for a touch of ombudsmanry without being pure ombudsmen themselves. They will intercede with line superiors, plead causes, and attempt whenever possible to make up for the imperfections of bosses.

Somewhat less rare but nonetheless interesting are the assignments of management development and organization development people.

The management development people help plan the progress of managers and potential managers. They try to develop answers to that persistent query, "Whom are we grooming for top management in the future?" Management manpower planning and development are clearly in the hands of such people. M.B.A.'s and other advanced degrees are crucial.

Another set of few but mighty jobs for advanced-degree holders lies in an area called organization development or "O.D.," as it is sometimes known. Such M.B.A. and Ph.D. types help companies develop organization structures along the lines advocated by business school research and theory.

CHAPTER 9

A MONTH IN THE LIFE
OF A PERSONNEL SPECIALIST

APRIL seemed a busy year for Charles Jenks. As assistant personnel manager for T. & H. Printing Company, he had been exposed to a greater variety of projects and problems than he had ever imagined could exist in a relatively small company and be solved by one relatively small man.

T. & H. specializes in catalog and magazine printing. Total sales were $50 million last year on a national basis. Charles worked at the headquarters plant in Pittsburgh. He had joined the company two years before after an undergraduate business program, majoring in business economics and behavioral sciences.

The month of April had been launched with a bang when his boss, the personnel manager, had called Charles in and said, "I want you to meet with the union shop steward at the Kentucky plant tomorrow. His people have a grievance against a manager down there."

So Charles drove down to Kentucky and met with a committee of workers from the plant. An assistant plant superintendent was charged by the union members with consistently performing work with his own hands which was under the jurisdiction of union printers.

Charles' first act was to talk with the alleged culprit. "I suppose I'm guilty," admitted the superintendent. "On a couple of occasions, I have actually re-arranged type on a printing form. Every time it was late at night. No union compositors were around. We were up against a deadline and I wanted to get the forms on the press. Since I know the process thoroughly, I grabbed type with my own hands and put it into place. Trouble was that I got caught, so it turned out to be unwise. The union people have been slowing down at their work in protest, costing us thousands of dollars worth of delay."

Charles persuaded the manager to agree to keep his hands off type and sign an agreement to that effect. This placated the union people. Then he pointed the nose of his car northward to spend a day at a Pennsylvania state college, his alma mater, where he was going to interview 12 students for a job as a beginning salesperson for his company.

He enjoyed being back at alma mater, though he found his first set of on-campus interviews quite harrowing in that the half-hour interview was so short and the necessity of "playing God" was so difficult based on such brief and scant evidence. He was painfully aware also that he was only faintly older than the students he was judging. But he felt great about discovering two students, a woman and a man, to invite to Pittsburgh for further interviews.

As Charles traveled homeward from the college, he reflected that recruiting was symbolic of what he loved about his work. The element of helping people lent a strong appeal. He felt he had added to the education of the 12 students he had interviewed, even though he had screened out 10 of them. Some had had good questions and he felt he had aided them in getting a grip on the world.

Charles had always mistrusted the people who made a big deal about loving everybody and thus wanting to help them all. Still he recognized a streak of altruism in himself.

As with most good jobs, he reasoned, the work was fine, the people were often appealing, but there were too many of them and too little time. He sighed as he steered into his driveway.

The following week, Charles was thrown a pair of tough problems by his boss. The first was presented by a middle-aged man, a shop foreman. Looking gray-faced and haggard, the older man sat before Charles with eyes downcast, twirling his cap nervously in his hands.

"I've had a bad absentee record lately," the man said. "You guys must have noticed. I've finally faced up to the fact that I'm a drunk and need some help."

Then followed a harrowing recital of bottles stashed in his desk, of a quart of whiskey consumed in a day, of an uncertain and harried life, in which the foreman was nipping on his bottle every half hour, trying to hide the habit from his wife, friends, subordinates. He gradually reached the point where he couldn't function, couldn't concentrate. Finally he was turning to his company for help.

"That's rather unusual," Charles' boss told him. "Too many people are afraid they'll lose their jobs if they 'fess up to their difficulties. Actually, the National Council on Alcoholism and Alcohol Abuse tells us we can expect that one out of ten workers has an acute alcohol problem."

Charles subsequently brought in a state official charged with fighting industrial alcoholism to meet with the foreman to help him both "dry out" and "kick the habit."

A few days later, the boss called him again. "Now you're going to get a taste of the ombudsman role. Frequently we have to listen to complaints from our people about their bosses and naturally we want to keep the matter confidential, so the boss doesn't take it out on the complainant."

Charles heard out the complaint. A young black accountant was upset because his passing of the certified public accounting examination had not resulted in his getting the promotion he figured was his due.

"I worked hard, took the special C.P.A. review course, and I passed with flying colors," he said. "That was six months ago. The chief auditor and the controller both knew about it. Do you think they said a word? No. I wanted some stroking, sure, but more than that, I feel I should have been promoted to senior auditor. I want a better job and I need the money. After all, I've got a family to feed. Hanging the C.P.A. certificate on the wall just doesn't do the trick."

Charles shook his head in agreement. I'll see what I can do without rocking the boat too much, he promised himself.

But he did have to rock the boat a bit. He talked to the chief auditor, who commented, "C.P.A. or no C.P.A., he's the same guy he was before he passed the exams. Why, he's only been here two years and it took me six years to make the rank he now wants!"

Charles wanted to say something fast and smart in rejoinder, but he held his tongue and tried to keep cool. He replied, "Sure, Mr. Venema, but times have changed. I think we have to recognize that the C.P.A. does carry weight in the job market. You know, this fellow is a hot item. Other companies will grab him up fast for a better job and more money."

They left it that way, but a week later, Mr. Venema called to say that he'd talked it over with the controller and they'd both agreed to promote the young C.P.A. In talking the matter over with his own boss, Charles suggested that they ought to put a red tag on the employment file of every person known to be undertaking some self-improvement through part-time schooling. He pointed out that in most cases this would be easy to do, because the company offers a tuition refund plan for most such study.

"Good idea. Why don't you implement the plan, Charlie? And speaking of study, we need to develop some kind of company orientation classes for all those new clerical employees we're hiring. Give that a little study, too."

Charles grinned and pulled on his ear. Both projects sounded like fun, but when would he find time? But all he said was, "Okay, John, okay."

CHAPTER 10

SALES, THE FRONT LINE OF BUSINESS

EMPLOYERS OFTEN COMMENT about the reluctance of college graduates to enter sales and some other aspects of marketing. Some explain this as the same sort of reluctance a soldier might feel about being sent to the front lines. For, in truth, the sale or movement of products and services is the front line of business. Without ability to sell a product, all the rest of the business equation is empty. The machinery, the buildings, the factory workers, the computers, the finance and accounting, all go for nothing if the products cannot be sold.

Robert Calvin, a Chicago management consultant to distressed businesses, maintains that it is lack of marketing acumen that causes most businesses to go under, rather than lack of financial capital.

Starting at the very firing line, then, the basic job is that of the foot soldier, the salesperson. This individual may be called other things—marketing representative, account representative, account executive, sales engineer—but basically the job involves calling upon both new and present customers.

There is a strain running through modern culture which renders sales jobs suspect to educated young people. Some of it may be a carryover from Graeco-Roman, early Christian, Medieval and Renaissance times when people who sold goods they had not made themselves were regarded as socially less than desirable, or as usurers, people who charged unwarrantedly high interest on money. Selling has been a much lower caste profession than it deserves to be, considering its economic contribution.

Viewed in the light also of their professional demands, sales jobs of the sorts that are rewarding to college graduates call for considerable knowledge, education, aptitude, and skill.

On the knowledge score, the salesperson of a relatively complex product must be equipped to understand the product thoroughly, more thoroughly than any of the customers.

The salesperson must also have the sensitivity to sense the customer's concerns, buttressed by the knowledge of how the customer's business operates, for it is only by knowing where and how one's product can meet these needs that the salesperson will make a sale.

Take a salesman of printing presses. He may well be a mechanical engineer. He must be able to spot how a new, million-dollar piece of equipment, a giant offset printing press, can be an essential ingredient in improving the profitability of a new printing plant. He must be able to wrestle with some intimacy with the problems faced by his customer.

The saleswoman of computer equipment, one of the more common and rewarding of the collegiate sales jobs, is not really selling or leasing machinery so much as she is selling a system. It is a system for keeping accounts, or for controlling machines, or controlling supplies. She must understand accounting, production, and inventory control, to convince her prospects to install her company's computers.

It can be truly said that such salespeople are management consultants offering advice and counsel to their clients, and, in turn, selling their products as part of the solution.

The long-standing relationships between one company and another, between a supplier of leather hides to a shoe factory or a supplier of batteries to an automobile manufacturer, are kept alive by high-level salespeople, who render workable supply arrangements with customers.

At once an advantage and a drawback of selling jobs is that they may be based partially or wholly upon commission. For some salespeople this means there is virtually no limit, other than taxes, on income. In some companies, there are salespeople who regularly make more money a year than the officers. On the other hand, dependence on commissions can offer quite sparse recompense for weak salespeople or those in a sluggish market.

Goods do not automatically grace supermarket shelves. They are there in part because salespeople from the manufacturers, processors, and packagers have been calling upon store buyers and managers, "pushing" their wares and brands. Often such salespeople will "stock" the shelves themselves, trying to secure favorable positions for their own brands.

The large number of Americans who own stocks or bonds can be traced to "salesmanship." The same is true of insurance, particularly life insurance. The missionary zeal of life insurance salespeople is supportable. They have indeed saved the financial lives of millions of people.

In short, the American standard of living is largely dependent upon the ability of salespeople to sell autos, refrigerators, travel, books.

The occupation or profession of selling can be an end in itself; it can provide such consummate monetary reward that the salesperson is satisfied with it for a working lifetime. Making a sale provides other satisfactions too. Sometimes they are atavistic, that is, a throwback to the thrills of the chase, the hunt, the military conquest—preoccupations of our ancestors for centuries.

As one achieving sales giant put it:

"As I look back on my career, I have found nothing to equal the kick I get out of the sale of new business. It beats my favorite sport, fishing. In fishing, there is that unknown and unseen creature down there in the water. In selling, you know what is down there. You can plan, prepare for the catch, which makes it all the more thrilling when you land him.

"My wife always knew when I came home and had made a substantial new sale. She said my eyes shone with a special pleasure and a vibrance."

In addition, in a selling job well done there is the satisfaction of providing a service in which one believes. If there is a common trait shared by successful salespeople, it is their ability to believe completely in a product. Such people are frequently both inspired and inspiring.

One of the world's greater salespersons has said, "If you can sell, you will never lack a job." And that is true, as a look at the help wanted ads during an economic recession will show you. Good salespeople are always needed, never expendable.

As my father used to say, "The only irreplaceable man is the man who controls business, the man who has his own customers in his pocket. He is indispensable."

And it is true that people bearing other titles are in truth business-controlling salespeople. Many a partner of a law firm, a management consulting firm, an accounting firm, is a prime salesperson who holds the major clients of the partnership in his or her own pockets.

Marketing has been alluded to as being a "line" set of occupations, and certainly this is true of sales. For those who wish to use sales as a stepping stone into other realms, it provides a ready upward access. There are hundreds of higher executives, including presidents, who started out in sales. There is a tendency in the marketing hierarchy of many industrial companies to consider any person who has not been "in the field," i.e. a salesperson, as someone who is not a full-fledged marketing professional.

Just as a general in the Air Force will have "won his wings" by piloting planes in his earlier days, so a marketing executive will likely have similarly "won his feet" on a sales beat.

As one top sales manager put it, "My people will never completely trust someone who has never had boots muddied from calling on customers and has never had the eerie experience of turning a cold door knob to face a prospect never seen before."

To earn the cameraderie of the feet, to be a salesperson of either the career or "on the way up" variety, what are the traits of personality that are needed? For one thing, sales jobs of the sort we're discussing do not call for slam-bang, super-extroverts filled with racy stories and equipped with few brains, a shoe-shine, and a smile. The days of Willy Loman, the traveling salesman, the pitchman, the drummer, are largely gone.

Companies hiring collegians into jobs selling complex machines or services look for adequate personalities, of course. If not extreme extroverts, companies want people who are not shy, who can communicate effectively with other people, and who have enough courage and self-assurance to be able to handle rebuffs. They are not going to make all the sales they attempt and they can't expect to be loved or even tolerated by all people. But they know if they make enough calls, they will make enough sales.

Sales managements tend to have developed workable sales training programs. They feel that a fair percentage of people can be made into effective salespeople. However, people who are shy, retiring, ill at ease with others, or just plain reluctant to give of themselves are wise to steer around selling careers. On that latter score, people who consider it demeaning to have to court other people are going to be neither happy nor successful at sales.

Quite naturally, the ranks of sales executives are drawn almost exclusively from salespeople. One of the principal routes into marketing management, particularly with companies selling industrial products, is to come up through the sales management ranks.

Companies and industries vary in the way sales territories and managerial responsibilities are divided up. Most typically, the first-rung sales executive has charge of a few salespeople in a relatively restricted territory, a county, or a city. Next step will be to head a state or a large metropolitan area, then a region, and then on to nation-wide responsibility.

The most successful salespeople do not necessarily make the best sales managers, although quite naturally people with the best sales records tend to attract notice. Selling and management call for somewhat different sets of muscles. Good salespeople have to be superb at managing their own time, directing their own efforts, honing their own style. Successful salespeople in the same company often vary all over the lot in personal style. Independence and mastery over one's own time are attractive features of the sales role.

However, successful management of self is a different proposition from successful management of others. Sales management calls for transferring energy to helping others succeed at selling. This is often a very hard thing for egocentric and charismatic salespeople to do.

Good actors are not necessarily successful as directors; star athletes are not always competent coaches; excellent musicians do not inevitably make excellent teachers or conductors. Here one sees the prima donna role translated into an outward-focused role of concern for nurturing others.

Sales managers epitomize the challenges to line managers. They must be concerned with others and train them patiently, listen to their complaints, slap their backs over their successes, constructively call attention to their weak points, console them over their failures. Selling is a role sometimes hard on the ego and salespeople must be encouraged to weather economic downturns and personal slumps with some equanimity.

Sales managers must somehow inspire their salespeople, fill them with a sense of mission for the product, the company, and concern for those many benighted prospects out there who have not seen the light. Coach, teacher, friend, boss, inspirer, sales managers are all of these things. They must learn to live as much for the success of others as for themselves, although obviously the two successes are intertwined.

It can be easily perceived why line sales managers need all the help they can get from their staffs. They need help with training, assigning territories, designing compensation plans, and incentives, carrying out contests, setting quotas.

Sales trainees, promotion people, compensation experts, marketing researchers, all these are behind-the-lines suppliers to the troops out front.

CHAPTER 11

A DAY IN THE LIFE OF A COMPUTER SALESPERSON

I WAS AWAKE before the alarm went off today. You can't blame me. This is what I'd been training for in the year since I left the university. First I went to a company school for many weeks to learn the uses of computers in business. Regular classes at a high level. Most of the others in the classes were M.B.A.'s like me—from all sorts of schools. The competition was stiff.

Then I was assigned to the downtown district in this city, to a unit which specializes in selling and leasing computers to banks, savings and loan associations, and insurance companies. For a few months now, I have been understudying with an experienced salesperson and an experienced technical expert or engineer. The technical expert is a graduate-degree-holder too. The two of them work as a team.

Much of the time, the lead salesperson and I call on current users of our machines. We inquire as to how things are going. If there are bugs in the machinery itself, we call in our engineer and some of his people to fix it.

Frequently my boss will arrange a training program for personnel of our client company. It's one thing to install a battery of computers and another to train the personnel to run them. Sometimes he trains small groups himself and he has given me a couple of chances to do that too. I never realized how much of a teacher a salesperson has to be. It's a big educational job all the way through. Frequently we'd call out training experts from the district office to do the job and, of course, our customers are continually sending their personnel back to our home office for training—usually a week at a time.

Well, my boss arranges all of these things, so you can see that salespeople have a heck of a lot more to do than just sell. But they are always selling too. When talking with current users, they are looking for chances to offer new machines or mechanical devices, or our own prepared ways of programming the computers. Salespeople help them and, of course, sell more of our company, and these two things are obviously the name of the game. By helping more, you sell more.

I enjoy the new business "pitches" most of all. Before we call "cold" on new prospects, we case them, that is, we find out everything about them we can in advance. It is my job to study the annual and interim financial reports of our target companies and brief my boss on them. Then we'll eyeball the place as best we can. In other words, we spend some time on the premises, watching all the operations that we can see.

We have spotters too. In most of the larger prospect companies, we have some people working who are "graduates" of our company and trained by it. They are almost always agreeable to providing us tips on how the place is run, what kinds of systems they use, what kinds of machines. You can usually count on prospects having problems. Naturally these make good bets for us. If they seem to be in good shape and doing a job, we limit ourselves to polite calls without any strong pitch for the business—for the time being.

But where we have any evidence of weakness, we really hit. We piece together the points of weakness from our scouting. Say we find that an insurance company is having a bad time processing incoming payments from policy holders. Like as not, my boss, having found out from the files, or talking to secretaries or to our alumni to determine who the right person to talk to would be, will walk right in and say to the guy, "I'll bet processing those premium checks is a nightmare." Chances are the other guy will roll up his eyeballs in his head and agree.

Then my boss has him. "We solved that problem for Acme down the street two years ago. Are you interested?" Interested, I'll say! Usually the other man is so eager to hear, he'll choke on his coffee.

Well, what's so special about today? It's that I get to make my own final presentation to an important new customer. We worked long and hard on the whole proposition. Our engineer brought in a lot of other engineers and some experts from the home office. I had to understand what they were talking about, because I had to direct the whole "dog and pony show," as we call it.

The prospect is a really big bank with umpteen branches all over the state. We got onto the fact that their central headquarters had not solved the problem of keeping track of the transactions of these local banks, even though it was very important for them to know every day just where they stood.

Well, we got their permission to work out a rough system for them for presentation today. It wasn't too hard, because our engineers had perfected a sharp system for a similar bank in another city.

So there I was today with a flip chart and a blackboard and a pointer, outlining our ideas to the heavy brass at the bank. Of course, my boss and the engineers were there to back me up, and I called on each of them in turn.

They were all great and the whole thing went smoothly. Oh, they asked some tough questions, particularly the operations V.P., who knows a lot about computers. But it turned out he'd once worked for our company, and I think we answered all of his questions.

We won't know for several weeks whether we'll get the job or not, because the whole thing has to go before the board of directors. I may have to appear before them too. Whatever happens, I know I did a good job today. When it was over, my boss shook my hand and patted me on the shoulder, and said, "Joe, you graduated today. I'm proud of you." He doesn't throw compliments around. Right now, I feel great!

CHAPTER 12

CONSUMER BRAND MANAGEMENT

FOR TWO GENERATIONS now the activities surrounding the promotion and sale of "package goods" has held a relatively glamorous draw for the college educated. This is easy to understand. The job of winning allegiance to this or that brand of food, soap, or related personal and household items is a demanding one. Competition is keen, buying motives are complex. The sales to the public are made through advertising which is something we all see and know through TV and other mass media.

For the many students who take academic work in economics, psychology, and sociology, or in the business fields of marketing and advertising, consumer marketing can have a strong appeal.

Why does the housewife prefer one brand over another? Is the package more appealing? When she warms up a frozen food, can she be made to feel good about herself, because she is cooking and hence less guilty about shortcutting her housework? Tons of academic and commercial research, much of it revealingly human, has been conducted over the years.

The products are small, relatively low-priced, but scarcely trivial when so much of comfort, convenience, nutrition, and personal confidence are dependent on them.

Fundamental or main line jobs in the consumer marketing hierarchy are those of product or brand managers. The titles will vary according to the companies. Young college or university graduates, most often M.B.A.'s, sometimes B.A.'s or other degree holders, begin at the lowest rung of the brand management hierarchy as brand assistants or marketing assistants. They have a good chance of moving upward through assistant brand manager, brand or product manager, marketing director with responsibility for several groups of brands, and general managers at the vice presidential level and above. Many times such people become chief executive officers of their companies.

Brand managers are in charge of running a business within a business, or a "profit center" as it is known. They have responsibility for profits or losses incurred by the brand. Brand managers are given a budget over which they may have little control. This lack of budgeting determination is a sore point with some brand managers, because brands do fail for inadequate "seed money" or investment.

Typical decisions involve sales functions, liaison with the production or manufacturing people as to how much product they should turn out and when, and similar relationships with the sales managers and selling forces who will be putting the goods onto retail store shelves.

Brand managers also are concerned with matters of package design, both from the point of view of aesthetics and practicality. And the effectiveness of the product is important. Does it do what the advertising says it does? Under current laws and practices governed by the Federal Trade Commission it must.

Advertising is a crucial concern of brand managers. They have the help of that unique professional outside organization, the advertising agency, in deciding what the design and content of the ads should be and where and how often the ads should be run, but the final decision in these matters will rest with the brand management people.

To help them with all these considerations, brand managers will have open to them the services of marketing research workers within their own company, within the advertising agency, or with outside firms whose sole business is marketing research. They are all dedicated to testing the market through various social scientific devices.

The relationship between brand managers, their assistants and the advertising agency executives is complementary. In many ways, they sit on opposite sides of the same desk. Resting on this desk is the brand in question and the advertising strategy which will be employed to "pull" that product through wholesale and retail channels by creating a consumer demand for the specific brand.

Virtually all of the advertising and marketing personnel with whom the brand manager will deal will hold college degrees.

CHAPTER 13

BRAND MANAGER MEETS MARKET RESEARCHER

CONNIE HUNG UP the phone and sat quietly for a while, digesting the news. She had just been promoted to assistant brand manager and faster than she had expected. But equally unexpected was the news that she had been assigned to a different product, a new product as yet unmarketed. That could be spooky.

You see, Connie had expected to be advanced on her present brand, a toothpaste. What did she know about shaving cream? That was to be her new brand. But, at least, George would be on the new brand, as manager. George had been assistant brand manager on the last assignment and the person more than anyone else responsible for her training.

What did she know about shaving cream? Connie ruefully scratched her chin. No whiskers there. She thought back on her first three months with the company, where she was assigned as a salesperson calling on retail stores. She was indeed selling shaving cream to store buyers and managers, along with toothpaste, but mostly she was filling orders and shelves without giving the products that much thought.

At her first meeting with her coworkers on the new account, the details of the new brand were unmasked. George handed a can of the product to each of them. "Push the button," he ordered. They did and out came white foam, but not just white—also hot. Connie was startled. She shook the can, looked at it upside down. Somebody muttered, "Must be a devil in there!" Then George introduced a company chemist who had perfected the invention. They were told that they were among the first people to witness the finished product.

Next day, the brand group met with the corporation marketing research people to talk about researching the cream to determine for sure that it would "fly." Connie was assigned to confer for a few hours with Michael and Beth, two young people from the research staff.

Michael had gone to the same business school as Connie, and Beth had majored in psychology at a big state university nearby.

"What do you folks on the brand want to know?" asked Beth.

"We want to know whether hot lather out of a can will appeal strongly enough to people to cause them to switch to our brand from other brands of shave cream, both ready-applied and brush and lather. We also want to know if it can help compete with the movement toward electric razors. Can moves in that direction be reversed?" replied Connie.

Michael opined that ascertaining such matters would be a fascinating project. "Don't know quite how we'd do it," he said, "but anyone with an interest in consumer psychology would love to help set up the research."

Beth then indicated that she had seen a reference to a research study in the *Journal of Marketing* that might have relevance. As she recalled it, there was a study made to determine what motivated a person to select one mode of shaving over others. The researchers were employed by an electric razor company that featured the speed of the shave as the most important appeal in their advertising.

The research, as Beth reported it, had been motivationally designed and conducted by skilled interviewers. The results were surprising in that a sizable number of those interviewed were not much concerned about speed or convenience. They liked the feel of lather and the excuse to spend time eyeing their favorite person in the mirror. They liked lathering white beards on their faces, looking wise and Jovian.

"Let's see if we can find that article in the company library," Connie said. She was beginning to get excited.

Next move would be to consult the marketing analysts to find how large the market for shaving cream is. What types of products and what brands have the leading share of that market? What would a logical price be? Where should it be distributed? Through what kinds of stores? These would be questions for the crew of market analysts down the hall.

And then, some of the questions being answered, there'd be the highly interesting sessions with the advertising agency.

CHAPTER 14

ADVERTISING—
THE LIBERAL ARTS OF BUSINESS

I AM IN ADVERTISING—not the "ad game" or "ad biz." I make that distinction because so much inaccurate and sensational claptrap has been written about advertising that I want to counteract it and make the point that advertising is a serious business, though, as with any other business, it has its fun for people who are appropriate for it.

I am 27 years old and college educated with English as an undergrad major and a Master of Science in Journalism degree with a speciality in advertising. I discovered early on in college that I am a better than average writer, so I took a cue from this and started in advertising as a writer—a copywriter, we call it in advertising.

For a couple of years I have written the verbal content of both print ads and TV commercials for a large advertising agency in a big city. It's hard work thinking up headlines and messages. The hardest work is trying to catch the speech of people, the kinds of people who read the ads. Many of them are not college graduates. Their speech and ages and backgrounds are different from mine and those of my friends and yet my job depended on my ability to communicate to these folks.

There aren't all that many professional jobs in the advertising business, but most of the people who go into them are college graduates. Some go with agencies. Agencies are sort of consulting firms which create advertising for their clients, those companies which manufacture and sell most of the goods we all buy.

Gradually as I worked with the agency I came to know the various other kinds of people who work on the ads. There are, for example, the media people or media buyers, as they are often known. These folks decide by careful statistical price and audience analysis whether the ads will be running in newspapers, magazines, TV, or radio, and what specific publications or stations should be used.

I work also with artists, often called layout people. They do the preliminary designs or the rough layouts called "storyboards" in TV. These sketches are where the ads start. Some ideas start with words, some with pictures. I learned at an early stage to think enough like an artist to get along with them. I now work pretty well as a teammate with artists. It's a neat trick for a word merchant to catch on to pictures.

I work under a copy chief who passes on my work to the creative director. He is higher up than the art director, who is at the same level of responsibility as a copy chief.

Well, these higherups pass on the words and pictures and ideas. Often we get the ideas from the research people, who are busy finding out what people want, what they'll react to, what will sell them.

You know ads and commercials can be clever, funny, beautiful, catchy, and can win all sorts of prizes in advertising competitions, but if they do not sell the goods, they are useless. Researchers are trying constantly to measure the effects of ads on consumer purchases. It's a complex business, knowing what affects sales. There are many variables. Researchers try to check movement of goods off store shelves and relate this to changes in the advertising. Of course, such elements as word of mouth and the weather creep in. Just about the only direct measure of ad sales power is in direct mail advertising where the ad is the only element involved in a sale.

As it was put long ago, advertising is salesmanship in print—or nowadays on film.

Speaking of salesmanship, some of the most important people I work with here are charged with selling our ideas for the ads themselves and the media and locations where they'll be run. These are the account executives or account representatives.

The account executive's job is to work with the brand managers at the client companies to determine the company's advertising needs and problems. The account executive in turn reports and translates these needs to me back at the agency. The account executive is the go-between, the translator, the person who has to look both ways, both at the advertising or communications side and the marketing side, the client's side.

Whatever else advertising is, it is marketing, communications, and a blend of both. The account people are the blenders. They offer both advertising and marketing advice to me in the agency and also to the client.

Sometimes we writers meet not only with our own account people, but with the representatives of the client. Sometimes the best place to generate ideas is in a room alone, staring at a blank sheet of paper. Other times it involves working with other people in a group to come up with a great idea that will last for years. Take that brilliant term which has positioned the soft drink, 7-UP. You know, they call it "the Uncola."

It's my understanding that this idea came out of a group "skull session." The account execs, the agency "creative" staff, artists and writers and the like were sitting around with the client people searching for a way to establish both a personality and a position for the drink—something to remove it from just another pop and to enable it to compete in the public imagination with Coke and Pepsi. That was a big order.

Someone was at the blackboard, writing down some of the brainstorming ideas. People were just letting it flow, spewing forth ideas quite randomly, trying to let their imaginations soar.

One person suggested that the drink be stressed as a relief from the colas for people tired of them. So the fellow at the board wrote down, "the anti-cola" and the "non-cola," along with dozens of other ideas that popped up.

Later in the session, the group went over all the things they had scribbled down. One by one they erased them or put them aside for further action. Finally, "non-cola" was left. "Too clumsy," someone said, "How about the Uncola." "Yeah, yeah," came the chorus. A terrific idea was born.

That person with the word must still feel great about it. Just great! I don't know whether he was a writer, an artist, an account exec, or a brand manager for 7-Up.

That's what I like about advertising. It's ideas. There are some allied fields, likewise filled with ideas that I find equally fascinating. Take public relations, for instance. There aren't too many jobs in it and what there are we journalism types grab, usually after working as newspaper reporters of some sort. Instead of operating through paid-for publication space or broadcast time as advertisers do, public relations people try to furnish worthwhile news about their company or its products to make the news media. If it's good, editors and broadcasters will use it, free, of course.

Like those of us in advertising, "P.R." people have to make graspable something hard to grasp. What is a corporation? It is a big non-graspable thing unless, through news stories or ads, you are able to make people grasp warmly some idea of what the corporation is that they buy from or work for. We are the handle makers and the best handles are made of useful information.

CHAPTER 15

PORTRAIT OF THE ARTIST AS RETAILER

Question. Henry, how did you pick retailing as your work site and isn't it a bit unusual for a young person to be so engaged?

Answer. Yes, it is. Until fairly recently, retailers were not hiring too many college people, let alone M.B.A.'s like myself. They now realize that they have to do so because retailing margins are small and good analytic skills and sharp pencils are needed. They are hiring undergrad business school types and B.A. graduates.

Q. Are these people in merchandising and buying?

A. Well, yes, most of them, but the big retailers need finance people working with the vast budgets and investments of the bigger stores and chains and they need a lot of accountants for the same purposes.

Q. What has been your biggest kick in the four years you've worked for a retailer?

A. There have been a lot of them. I guess every time I psyched out the market and made a correct buying decision, I've gotten the kind of charge that makes life worthwhile. But I guess my biggest high was selling rather than buying for our large retailing and mail order firm.

Q. You mean this is something you sold to the public?

A. No, no, something even more difficult than that. As you know, I've been working as assistant to the regional merchandise manager for children's clothing in the southeastern states. We've perfected a type of expensive blue jean which is superior to all rival brands and is the best value for the money of any of the products in our kids' line. Our problem was that it was selling too well.

Q. How could anything sell too well?

A. Because it was the kind of blue jean our retailers in the Southeast would carry. They were forgetting that not everybody will buy at the top. We were getting clobbered on more moderate priced jean lines by our rivals, since we were concentrating on the quality stuff. We were missing out on the broad share of the market and that is not our custom.

Q. Well, how could you cure this situation?

A. As luck would have it, my boss, who was to make a pitch on the medium-priced jeans to all of the managers in the South, was involved in a car accident just before the meeting. And, what do you know, he asked me to fill in for him. I knew it was a great opportunity, but it made me feel pretty rocky at the same time. But, as you can guess, I really had no choice, so I bellied up to it. I grabbed the next plane to Atlanta to address our Southern managers, a good-natured, but notoriously hard-nosed lot.

Q. Couldn't you use your boss's speech?

A. He had it in his head on the hospital bed and was too banged up to see me. He had put together some slides and opaques for overhead projectors, but they were lying scattered out on the thruway in his wrecked car. I just stood up on my hind legs and gave it the old school try.

Q. Did you hit it head on?

A. Yeah, I cited statistics on our increasing share of the market at the high priced end and our miserable showing in the middle and lower priced markets, which, being much larger, are more profitable. They hollered a bit about crazy ideas from guys sitting in comfort at headquarters, but when I came to the research evidence showing that there wasn't too much "trade up" by price-conscious buyers to the good stuff, their arguments that they were converting cheapskates to high buyers collapsed. Before I was through, they were eating out of my hand and eagerly listening to our advertising and promotion items designed to insure them almost the whole market, not just the cushy stuff. I got more than a kick out of it! I got a promotion soon after.

CHAPTER 16

ACCOUNTING,
A FUNDAMENTAL SOURCE OF JOBS

WHETHER with a public accounting firm, an industrial firm, a financial or nonprofit institution, or government bureau, accounting represents a basic and fundamental source of jobs. At least half of all accountants work outside the accounting firms, and many get their starts right out of college.

Some of these people eventually study for the C.P.A. examination and others do not. Passing the C.P.A. is generally optional outside the public accounting profession, but its grounding can be valuable for anyone engaged in accounting activity.

While there are some companies which claim a preference for developing their own accountants rather than taking those already trained by C.P.A. firms, most organizations will use some from both sources.

Bookkeeping or recordkeeping has been practiced at least since the days of the Babylonians. Modern accounting—public, industrial, or institutional—regards itself as a far cry from past practice. It is a multidisciplinary profession. Today's accountant has effective resource allocation as a basic theme but is also involved in technical assistance in policy formation; design of management information systems; evaluation of results, personnel operations, financial systems, and social goals; improvement in performance in relation to standards, computing systems, and changing conditions; and assistance in the design of planning and control activities.

Most young people start as assistants in accounting departments, usually after having taken some accounting or business courses. A knowledge of accounting is fundamental to any type of business activity, be it banking and credit, investment, or manufacturing.

Some beginning company accountants eventually work their way into internal auditing, a term usually implying that there is some spot internal inspection and control of every sector of a company's activity.

An internal auditor is very much like an inspector general in the Army or a federal or state bank examiner. You never know when these people are going to show up and ask not only to see the books, but to review the entire operation—on the spot. The spotcheck is one of the most effective methods ever devised for keeping people on their toes against the day of actual inspection.

Call them accountants or auditors, people in these general areas like to call their function "control," referring to establishment of appropriate systems of checks and balances. They then come up the controller's or comptroller's (the words are interchangeable) route. The chief financial officers of many corporations developed this way.

There has been a change in the role of industrial accountants as they have switched from an emphasis on budgeting and reporting to activity in planning and forecasting. Corporation accountants are indeed considerably more of a generalist financial functionary than they used to be.

Public accounting is the most professional of business pursuits in that it demands formal certification for its practice. The top 25 public accounting firms are the most prestigious identifiable hirers of college talent, each year taking on at least 20,000 college graduates. They provide a set of jobs that simply cannot be ignored by college graduates with a penchant for business. Public accountants comprise 41% of all people engaged in accounting, the others serving as accountants with corporations, institutions, and government bodies. Over one-third of all public accountants work for the "Big Eight," the eight largest accounting firms.

Public accounting firms utilize accounting majors from undergraduate schools as the principal source of their hires, although they often are willing to convert other types of business majors and undergraduates from social sciences and the arts. An increasing number of liberal arts schools are offering some accounting courses to their undergraduates, a practice much appreciated by accounting firms. An increasing number of those hired by the public accountants are M.B.A.'s, or people with the more specialized Master of Science in Accounting degree. As high as 40% of those hired by the major accounting firms hold advanced degrees. This is in recognition of the complexities of American economic life which places more and more stress on the highly educated accountant.

The 125,000 members of the American Institute of Public Accountants are college graduates who passed a rigorous examination prepared and graded by the Institute. They have also satisfied certain experience requirements and then been issued a license to practice in a state.

The C.P.A. is engaged in a variety of activities, working variously as an auditor, a tax advisor, an accountant, or as a management consultant.

In their service as auditors, C.P.A.'s meet requirements for the 5,000 publicly held companies which are required by law to have certified audits yearly to protect their 32 million stockholders.

Some 90% of the audits and related services are conducted by the "Big Eight" firms. These audits are by no means limited to the publicly held corporations. Smaller firms and other privately held corporations are provided accounting statements useful for seeking bank loans or undertaking reorganizations, or generally for decision-making purposes. Non-profit and governmental agencies also retain public accountants. Auditing is a process of testing the propriety of financial statements which are a combination of facts, judgments, estimates, and related information concerning financial position and operating results.

Audits start with a careful look at a company's internal control system for accuracy and possible dishonesty. An auditor is careful to observe employees at work. Sampling techniques are used to test transactions, scrutinize documents, and compare receipts to company records. Suspicions of irregularities lead to deeper searches.

Working in teams, auditors compare bank balances, spot-check outstanding bills to determine probability of payment and examine the procedures for counting, then valuing inventory. The process continues with auditors tallying marketable securities, reading minutes of meetings, studying contracts, and talking with myriad people about company operations.

At the end of this long process, the auditor reaches a conclusion and reports it. This is the final step, the bottom line in the report.

The C.P.A. as tax advisor serves in a separate tax cadre within the firm. This is an area of business where a law degree can be helpful and a fair number of joint degree holders of the J.D.-M.B.A. combination, for example, are to be found in tax departments.

Obviously, helping individuals and businesses prepare tax returns is crucial to our society. It is complex, subject to change, essential.

Typically, the new hire with an interest in taxes will start as an auditor for a C.P.A. firm and eventually branch into taxes.

Also customarily starting with accounting firms in the audit category are those college graduates who will go into the management services or consulting sector with the accounting firms. Older students, most particularly M.B.A. candidates with some work experience, may go right into management consulting. Experienced people in the computer area are drawn upon heavily for this function. Almost invariably they hold advanced degrees.

Inevitably a great deal of the consulting work done by accounting firms lies pretty close to the audit and involves accounting systems. The spectrum of what consulting areas the firm will get involved in does range, however, from systems consulting at the conservative end of the spectrum all the way over to consulting on marketing, personnel, and production problems.

CHAPTER 17

A FORK IN THE ROAD
FOR A YOUNG CPA

MARY BRODY wouldn't get much sleep this night and she knew it. Her husband, Harold, knew it too. So they sat up late the way they often did during their school days, slowly sipping beer and having a "talk-over," as they called such occasions. Their subject was the job offer about which Mary had to make up her mind quite soon.

Mary had only recently passed the C.P.A. examination, a source of elation to both of them, and a fact of absolute importance to her career. A member of a "Big Eight" staff, Mary had known that her next promotion was quite dependent on her passing the test.

"Well, honey," Mary was saying, "whatever else I've gotten out of this job, the C.P.A. education was worth it. Look, already it's gotten me a swell job with a client."

"Well, you earned it; as a matter of fact, we both earned it. During the last two heavy seasons, you worked day and night, either on clients' business or studying for that exam. I almost forgot what you looked like. If you take that corporate job as assistant to the controller, you'll probably work a more human schedule."

"Probably." Mary replied. "But that depends on the controller's habits. He does seem a reasonable guy and the money is sure better—at least in the short run."

"Yeah, but we're going to live a long time. I'm not too sure just what your long-run prospects are with the accounting firm."

"You'd never listen when I tried to tell you. You always said the titles were funky. But I'll review the bidding for you. I am now a semi-senior accountant, which means I'm in charge of some audits with a couple of people under me. The junior accountant days are past, thank God. I've been crammed with knowledge and will probably be promoted to senior accountant soon. Maybe I can get into management services, but I haven't made my mind up whether I want to ask."

"Of course, for you accountants, becoming a partner is your Nirvana, your reward in heaven, isn't it?" Harold asked.

"Well, yes, and I think I'm on the kind of track where in seven years I might expect that. Once I pass that point, it'll mean $60,000 a year or better. I can scarcely expect to surpass that in the corporate world in that period of time. Of course, maybe I won't make partner. Only about 10% of those who start out in public accounting ever do, you know. We've got the old up or out policy. If I waited for another couple of years as a supervisor, it would all become clearer. As a supervisor, I'd probably be able to make a switch to the client side at a better level. As a manager, I'll have less day-to-day-grind, less dog work, more liaison between client and partner. It's a pretty good deal, but no cinch either."

"It all sounds pretty good to me from here on," Harold commented. "Funny, you and I have often talked about what I like or don't like about the bank, but not much about you and the accounting firm."

"Yeah, that's true and I guess I haven't even thought about it much—till now. Most of it I've liked. I don't mind auditing, but I don't love it. It does, in a way, appeal to my orderly mind—a lot more orderly than my house."

Harold smiled. "I hope you haven't liked the travel part too much," he said.

"Well, I haven't liked being away from you, if that's what you're driving at, but there hasn't been too much of that. Mainly that one assignment a year ago. Most of the other assignments haven't taken me away more than one night at a time. No, it hasn't been the travel so much as some sense of disembodiment, of having no face. An auditor is out there in a client's office a good part of the time, sitting at a borrowed desk, wrestling with somebody else's business problems. As you know, I've just got a little desk at our office, in with some other auditors. As yet, I have no sense of permanence about the job, even though I've been there three years. In the corporate job, I think I'd find a home, a sense of permanence, of mission to one company, if you know what I mean."

"I know what you mean, all right. But wherever you go, you can't help but feel permanent. After all, they need you; you count as a woman."

Mary threw one of the couch pillows at him—rather a hard throw at that.

CHAPTER 18

FIRST-YEAR DIARY OF AN AUDITOR

AN IMPRESSION of the pace of an initial year of work with a major accounting firm can be gained from this first-year diary[1] prepared by a young man in the employ of Coopers & Lybrand.

July 13. My first day at work! I completed employment forms, became acquainted with firm policy and procedures, and met with the assignment manager to discuss my upcoming assignments.

July 16–27. Attended the firm's core course on a college campus in southern California.

July 30–August 17. My first assignment, a stereo component manufacturer. I worked with an experienced person in analysis of accounts receivable and fixed assets, and on development of the client's investment tax credit.

August 13. Attended a planning session for a large timber and natural resources corporation audit. Engagement goals were outlined, potential problems identified, and our audit approach reviewed and discussed.

August 20–24. Assigned to assist a senior in the examination of a labor union's six-month financial statements.

August 27–September 7. Began work on the timber and natural resources corporation audit. Reviewed and tested procedures for payable and cash reconciliation systems. My work revealed that our year-end validation could be reduced because of effective internal control systems.

September 10–October 2. Assisted in "return on investment" simulations and analyzed policy-holder dividends for an insurance company client.

October 3–5. Helped with examination of a joint venture termination agreement. As a result of the investigation, our client recovered substantial cost overcharges made by the other party.

---

[1] From *Exit the Green Eyeshade*, Coopers & Lybrand's recruiting brochure, published by Coopers & Lybrand, the international accounting firm.

October 8–12. In preparation for the year-end audit of a construction company, I completed a sales system analysis.

October 15–November 2. Analyzed dividend distribution and compliance with SEC regulations for a mutual fund.

November 4. Was asked by the partners to assist in hosting the annual international partners' meeting held this year in San Francisco. I helped with the hospitality room and answered visitors' questions.

November 5–9. At the headquarters of a retail clothing chain, a senior and I performed tests of a new computerized accounts receivable system.

November 12–23. Worked on the audit of a national charity's local chapter. As this was a brand new client, it provided an opportunity to present complete documentation, such as a set of systems flow charts detailing their revenue/billing cycle.

November 26–December 31. Returned for year-end audit of the retail clothing chain and performed validation tests on various balance sheet accounts. I also utilized our firm-developed computer program and time-sharing terminal for computing footnote lease disclosure data.

December 10–21. In auditing a small client, the senior and I discovered what looked like unethical business practices in regard to a bank loan agreement. We called this to the attention of the partner and manager in charge who, after conferring with the client and the bank, decided to dissociate the firm from the engagement.

December 26–28. Took some of my accumulated overtime in days off. (Went skiing!)

January 2–25. Returned to the timber and natural resources corporation. I assisted in validating 12/31 account balances and conducted a procedural review of their computerized inventory-control system.

January 28–February 8. For the audit of a small nonprofit home health agency, I did almost all of the field work myself, with a senior reviewing my completed work papers.

February 11–25. Returned for year-end audit at the construction company where I performed validation tests of balance sheet accounts.

February 26–March 1. Performed physical inventory for a security service firm through "on-site" visits to the Bay Area branches of this New York office client.

March 4–29. Returned to the audit of a mutual fund. I reviewed and tested the security buy and sell procedures and helped in validation of the investment portfolio and preparation of the annual report.

April 1–5. Asked for and received a week's assignment to the tax department to gain experience in individual income tax preparation.

April 8–12. Took one week of my vacation.

April 15. Talked with several college students, answered their questions about the firm and chronicled my work assignments to date.

April 16–26. Was assigned, with complete responsibility, to audit and prepare tax returns for two pension funds of an automobile association.

April 25. Attended our office's annual staff golf and tennis outing.

April 29. My promotion to Staff A, effective May 1, was announced.

April 29–May 17. Returned to the automobile association to answer review notes on my previous work, to do a profit and loss fluctuation review, and to prepare their corporate tax return for review by the tax specialist.

May 3–7. Took time off to study for the upcoming C.P.A. exam.

May 8–10. Sat for the C.P.A. exam.

May 20–31. Audited the financial statements of an automobile insurance company's profit-sharing trust fund and drafted the entire financial report, including footnotes.

June 3–28. Spent four weeks in Los Angeles where I, as part of a five-member team, examined the revenue cycle of a large public utility and reviewed consolidated statements and reports to stockholders, the Federal Power Commission, and the SEC. Our findings were discussed with the client in an "exit" conference.

July 1–5. Took my second week of vacation.

July 8–12. Assigned to interim audit of an electronics company. In performing procedural review of the cost system at my location, I toured the manufacturing operation and computer center to see the interrelationship of operations and paperwork flow.

July 15. Attended an "in-house" class and discussion group—a session bound to prove valuable in future financial statement preparations.

July 16–August 15. With assistance, I performed the audit of a small private college. As a result of our work, the client discovered that it was in breach of certain covenants of the original endowment. A court order allowing the actions was applied for and granted.

CHAPTER 19

UNDER THE BROAD BLANKET OF FINANCE

"FINANCE" is even a broader word than "marketing" in that the term can be applied to just about everything that has to do with financial health and to the various financial institutions which serve corporations and governments. There are several gray areas into which finance jobs shade. At one end of the spectrum, for example, some companies may call a job "financial analysis," where virtually the same set of duties will be called "accounting" by some other firm.

Similarly the chief financial officer of a company may be called vice-president and controller, an accounting sounding title, or vice-president of finance. Typically, however, the chief financial officer does have a title which transcends the control or accounting factors. On the other end of the finance spectrum, the investment end, the chief financial officer may also be the treasurer. More typically, however, the chief financial officer's post transcends treasury as it transcends accounting control and covers both.

The finance job spectrum, then, might be simplified to look like this:

accounting related-financial analytic-financial planning-treasury

Financial analytic and financial planning jobs will look both ways—toward acccounting and investment and toward money management, having the middle necessity to be informed by both ends.

A rise into top management (i.e., chief financial or presidential roles) could come through any or all of these routes, so important is the financial side of business today.

The fact that majoring in finance is tremendously popular with undergraduate and graduate business school majors has been alluded to previously. A principal reason is undoubtedly that there are so many good jobs offered in the area. Part of the explanation for that may lie in the fact that financial jobs are complex. The liberal arts or science major can be trained for them by a company, but at a greater time and money expenditure than many companies are willing to invest.

Another factor already mentioned is that business school faculties through their research have devised methods, techniques, and philosophies of finance that have been of direct and indirect (through their students) worth to the world of practical business.

Business school graduates probably can be accused of seeing the world through green, money-tinted glasses, but there is no doubt that finance jobs represent an important segment for young people.

Here is the testimony of a financial analyst, one year out, about his job. While the duties of a financial analyst, a common entry-level post in corporations, do vary from company to company, his experience may be taken as broadly typical.

"You may not understand all of the specialized language in my account, but neither did I at first and neither does anyone who starts on a new job of a reasonably complex nature. A simplified description is impossible.

"I was hired with the title of financial analyst and told that I was in the vice-president and controller's group assigned to the funds analysis and special studies department, reporting to the manager of that department. I was handed a slip of paper which purported to summarize my first-year assignment. It read:

'The position involves projecting corporate cash flows, determining cash flows, determining cash requirements, establishing optimum inventory levels, administration of the corporate capital budget, acquisition and divestiture analysis, and special financial studies. The special studies cover such diverse areas as return on investment, calculations for proposed capital expenditures, lease versus buy decisions, manufacture versus purchase decisions, and financial analysis of comparable companies in our industry.'

"I was told that after my first assignment, my career path would be to a department manager position, a division marketing controller, or a position within the treasurer's department.

"My kind of job was usually entry level for an M.B.A. or open to a graduate of an undergraduate business school with a bit of age and experience.

"I soon found out what I probably should have suspected: comparatively few training programs are well worked out. They often involve much clerical work for which comparatively little education would be involved.

"But most of it was interesting enough to keep me going. At the heart of my job lay the collection, collation, and analysis of profit plan data, comparing net sales to net profit on a monthly basis. This matching of components is computerized in our fairly advanced company. I'd horse with it first manually and then put it on computer for checking. Usually I found something wrong.

"Sometimes I have gotten involved with treasury activity. I'd monitor capital investment procedures in financial services, capital expenditure proposals, and investment proposals. I always asked questions about the proposals. You know, self-seekers will not always put together honest proposals. We evaluate the success of accepted proposals for five years after they are made.

"I have found that I have some kind of an internal necessity to understand what the numbers represent and why I am working with them. I suspect this is the essential urge that differentiates a staff manager from a glorified clerk, this urge, this necessity to know. It serves you well when some big brass asks you to explain them and I have happily for my future, had some exposure to the top.

"My concerns have fortunately not been limited to finance. Though officially I may be called a 'financial analyst,' I could as easily be referred to as a 'planner,' without at all limiting that function to finance only. I have evaluated new products and existing products. To do this, I have been right in with marketing people and at other times I have needed to deal with the production people.

"I gain the impression from some of my friends in other corporations that their work is involved principally with data retrieval, data investigation, and working up costs. Many of us have functions very close to those of an auditor. Certainly my knowledge of accounting has been found wanting. I should have taken more of it and paid more attention to it in business school. Certainly a strong academic knowledge of finance is indicated and I have been able to make use of an early interest in computer modeling.

"As for getting ahead, well, I suppose that's always at the forefront of every young hot shot's mind. I guess I've determined that one must be creative. By that I mean that you must find out ways to turn out work that will be noticed. Limiting yourself to the routine stuff you are ordered to do will win you few plaudits. It is simply expected that you will be good at what you do as a professional. So you look for interesting approaches to presenting new, or even old, data in new forms. If your boss will pass it on up, and sometimes he will not because he is jealous and a little afraid of you, you may achieve visibility.

"A lot depends on your boss and his willingness to bring you along. I have at times been forced to go over the head of my immediate boss, but that is not a good practice, and I have been criticized for it in official reviews of my performance.

"I guess ultimately one learns that out there in life, nobody is as interested in your career progression as you are. You have to somehow manage to stand out and push your own cause. It isn't like school where high grades can be enough."

CHAPTER 20

BANKS AND SAVINGS AND LOANS

A HIGH PROPORTION of the jobs offered each year to college graduates are made by the financial institutions of the land—commercial banks, savings and loans, credit unions, and mortgage banks.

Another very large chunk of jobs rests in insurance, a vast, varied industry. Then there are the investment banks and stock brokerage firms and a much smaller set of opportunities in investment advisory services.

Each of these categories offers entry-level positions for those with bachelor's degrees of any sort, though the more technically complex or demanding jobs may call for the M.B.A. or a similar advanced degree. A number of the persons who enter these fields at the B.A. level do elect, often under employer sponsorship, to go on for advanced degree work in business or related areas.

In banking, the so-called commercial lending jobs have long been on the main line—that is, they are both the fastest track to promotion and the closest to the heart of the main business of the bank. Commercial lending has constituted the most common entry gate toward being president of the bank.

The major revenue base of the more substantial American banks lies in the loans they make to other businesses. The process of launching, arranging, and servicing these loans rests with the commercial lending people, many of whom are officers of the bank.

Banks have company officers in larger proportion to their staffs than any other type of commercial entity except possibly advertising agencies. Part of this is because the banks' business customers have more confidence in dealing with titled officials. Part of it is because bank officials need to be officers to have the power to make loans on their own without having to check at least the smaller generality of them with superiors singly or as a loan committee of the bank.

Loans are basic, but there are quite a few other kinds of services that the commercial lending officer proffers to customers. The bank will manage cash (show how to utilize money at the most advantageous rates), extend computer and communications facilities, and tender investment advice to its commercial customers.

Now these services do require selling, albeit usually on a dignified and consultative level. A commercial lending person in a bank is about as much a marketing executive as a finance executive. The finance comes in knowing credit, that is, in being able to assess whether the risk of bad credit is properly evaluated.

Banks are noted for offering superb training to college graduates in this very area of credit, training which occupies anywhere between six months to two years for new people. Such training, part of it quite formal, generally is mixed with on-the-job experience and is, in some instances, tied in with even more formal external schooling in graduate business schools.

As a result of the mix of good training and experience, bankers are often prized eventually for jobs on the corporate side of things, though many do find the very bank they start with an admirable site for a whole career.

Commercial lending can be applied domestically or internationally. Fundamentally, international banking is domestic lending applied on an international scale and complicated with differing rates of exchange, financial, accounting, business, and cultural customs. It calls for people with some claim to foreign cultural knowledge and experience and a great facility for quick adjustment to personal situations quite different from standard American.

The larger banks of the country seek M.B.A.'s for entry into their lending jobs, though some will launch B.A. and B.S. graduates. The first degree is usually enough for the medium-sized and smaller banks. The pay is good from the start with the larger establishments. However, except at the very top of the management pyramid, banks are not noted for the highest kind of pay. Some banks hire the B.A. graduate and sweeten the proposition with the perquisite of full tuition to a part-time M.B.A. program and occasionally some time released from work for reading and study for such a program.

Central as commercial lending may be to a commercial bank career, there are increasing opportunities for learning and advancement offered elsewhere within the banks. One such set lies in the growing emphasis on the "back room," that set of occupations known as "operations." The tellers in the "cages," the innumerable clerical func-

69

tionaries, the programmers, and other computer hands essential to the processing of bank transactions work in the operations area.

Bank officials are wont to point out that their profits on each transaction are actually relatively small. The transactional costs can make or break them. Most of such costs lie in the services of employees in the transactions. Bankers are given to point out that their inventory goes up and down on the elevators each night.

Traditionally the term "banker" has been reserved within banks for those involved in lending. Now it seems to include bank operations officers and some of the other non-lending categories within the bank.

Operations these days revolves heavily around the computer and quite naturally involves the kinds of persons who have training in that area and are likely to be able to develop and sustain interest in its challenges. Most of the banks' transactions are computer monitored, including the vast retail credit card business. The volume of check processing, even in a smallish bank, is staggering. Whereas all of the counting house aspects of banking in and out of the teller's station have not yet eliminated hand counting, we are on the way to such a state with our office machines.

Mention of tellers undoubtedly evokes what for most people is their image of the bank, namely as a local office dealing with the deposit of savings accounts, checking accounts, personal loans, home mortgages, and the like. In this respect, the large savings and loan industry is quite similar. Savings and loan organizations are retail by nature, providing savings systems for people and reinvesting these savings in mortgage loans to homeowners. Their internal operations bear similarity to those of banks.

Dealing with the consuming public is usually referred to as retail banking. It calls for skills in customer handling. There are good chances here for line leadership roles for college graduates. Many banks and savings and loans offer beginning jobs which are pointing eventually to running a local branch.

Banks and savings and loans are service marketers and as such offer jobs in advertising and marketing work. Much of this activity is representing the retail side where competition between the individual savings institutions is often intense and replete with gifts, premiums, and other incentives to placing one's money in one spot in preference to a second.

Local banks and savings and loans lend mortgage money and hence there are real estate-oriented jobs to be had. There are likewise investment cadres to invest the banks' funds in real estate and also in stocks, bonds, and other forms of investments.

The trust and investment sides provide their own sets of jobs. The trust department of a bank manages the funds entrusted to it by other people. Involved may be the estate of someone deceased. The commercial bank trust department is assigned the job of managing the money, the real estate, and perhaps the stock and bond investments for the heirs as well. They also manage the investments for institutions.

At one time the trust departments of banks were staffed largely by attorneys. While a certain number of lawyers are desirable, the mix has shifted and the preponderance of graduates being hired these days would hold degrees in the arts, social sciences, and business.

CHAPTER 21

"OUR BANK CAN BE USEFUL"

"OUR BANK can be useful in many, many ways." This Barry Johns found himself saying on a frosty January morning to the president of a small manufacturing company in a suburb of Minneapolis. It hadn't been easy to get in to see the president, but now that he was there, Barry felt pretty confident.

He was still glowing against the cold of the world because he had received at mid-year the significant promotion from lending assistant to lending officer. A graduate from one of the state universities a scant three years ago, his progress had been good because his bank was good and so was he.

"Well, what is it you can offer me that no other bank can offer?" the president asked. "I'm getting fast enough service on my loans as it is and what more can I ask?"

"I'd like our cash management people to talk with you," answered Barry. "You may have too much money lying around idle and drawing no interest."

"True, we may," answered the older man, "but I guess you ought to talk to our treasurer for that." Barry rose to this open invitation and did just that. The treasurer had not been much stimulated on that score by the two other banks the company dealt with and was interested in further exploration.

Barry next succeeded in arranging to have the president and the treasurer attend sessions offered to bank customers by the financial consulting arm of his bank. These people explained some of the latest methods of capital budgeting (allocating funds). They discussed investment theory, including a "random walk" thesis advanced by one of the business schools which had deduced from accumulated data on stock market prices that a random, rather than an "informed" selection of a portfolio with the aid of stock analysts, could have done just as well over the years.

One of Barry's friends, a young stock broker, railed against this theory and Barry arranged for his firm to argue the case before his customer company.

Barry's new client, a family-held company, was interested a few months later in exploring the possibility of "going public," that is, offering its stock to the public in order to obtain more financing.

The possibility of the corporate finance department of the bank helping out was explored, but it was limited by law in what it could do. As a consequence, Barry called in an investment bank, where a young classmate of his was working in corporate finance, the devising of ways to raise corporate funds, and a second classmate was engaged in underwriting, or distributing newly established stock issues to prospective buyers through a network of investment banking firms. The investment bankers examined other ways of financing and finally did recommend the issuance of new stock as opposed to other opportunities.

The investment banking network sold shares to institutions seeking to buy good stock investments through institutional salespeople and also through college-educated stock brokers who marketed the issue to individual buyers of stocks.

Barry had made himself and his bank useful to the new client.

CHAPTER 22

INVESTMENT BANKING, AN IMPORTANT CAREER FOR A FEW

INVESTMENT BANKING draws its recruits exclusively from the ranks of college graduates, offers higher income potential than many rival lines of work, and yet is very little understood by either collegians or their advisors.

There are several reasons for the mystery. This is not a large business in terms of numbers hired; it is relatively complex and its practitioners have not sought to be known beyond the world they serve. Also called the "securities industry" or "the street" (after Wall Street), people in the business refer to their varied pursuits as "investment banking." However you phrase it, theirs is an industry largely responsible for the financial capital raised to support United States business and industry, obviously a vital function.

Investment banking represents activity that partakes of both the marketing (selling) cluster of functions and of finance. The instruments sold and devised are inevitably financial. In this blending, it is not unlike its cousin, commercial banking.

Starting with what is often referred to as the income producing side, there are two principal kinds of sales activities carried on by investment banks. There are institutional sales to institutions, and individual or retail sales to members of the public.

Institutional and retail sales both concern themselves with two differentiated types of products, equities or stocks, and fixed income securities or bonds. On equities, there is no fixed rate of return guaranteed. On fixed income or debt items, represented by bonds, there is a fixed and predictable rate of return or debt owed the bond holder. Stockholders take their chances, but their rewards are potentially greater.

Though securities salespeople are offering both equity and fixed income to both institutions and individuals, institutions are limited by law as to what they can buy to a small amount of equities. Thus most institutional sales are concerned with fixed income items that are non-speculative. On the other hand, "retail" salespeople selling to individuals can run a wider gamut of offerings. This range includes stocks, convertible bonds, options, commodities, mutual funds, and annuity plans.

Before Securities and Exchange Commission regulations had been promulgated to force securities sellers to negotiate their sales commissions (as opposed to drawing fixed percentages), opportunities for making a great deal of money were traditionally better in institutional sales, because the volume was very high. This is less true today and a larger proportion of the more promising and ambitious brokers are in individual sales.

Most college graduates who enter the retail securities business eventually work on commission, some work on salary, some on a contract based on the profitability of the firm. Selling is done on the individual's initiative plus leads furnished by the firm as a result of inquiries, advertisements, and new business generated by accounts already in the house. A young person entering sales will usually spend four months to one year in training on salary and then stand for a brokerage examination in the individual's locality.

Though a sense of sales and marketing permeates all investment banks, there are some categories such as "corporate finance," which are not sales activities. Usually corporate finance people have M.B.A. degrees. They become involved in raising the investment money for the corporations, banks, and municipalities. They work with them to select what approaches they will take. They suggest plans and negotiate the mergers of one corporation with the next or the acquisition of one company by another, all in the interest of greater efficiencies and profits. They underwrite offerings of fixed income securities or equities to the public and institutions, buying large portions for their own firms and reselling them later through their own sales forces.

Whole groups or syndicates of investment banking firms will band together to offer new securities to the world. They also help arrange private placements of debt and transactions carried on by the two parties concerned without going through exchanges, the regular organized markets.

Corporate finance people may also serve as general investment advisors. College graduates in these pursuits are typically paid salary plus profit sharing, sometimes on a per deal basis.

THE MANAGERS

Another group within the firm is known as traders. They put the capital of the investment bank at risk in a variety of investments. This can be known as "taking a position" on new issues of stocks or bonds, but most of the investments by these firms are on the older issues. Trading serves to provide liquidity to the market and thus aids the clients of investment bankers.

In addition to these income-producing areas, there are support areas to these firms vital to the conduct of their own and their clients' business. Each of these provides jobs for college graduates at a considerable level of sophistication.

"Operations" covers all those jobs that have to do with the myriad details of each day's business. Records of who has bought and who has sold securities must be recorded and verified with the appropriate stock or commodities exchange.

Since 1968, when some of the firms were in trouble because of the comparatively loose manual handling of "back office" transactions, the procedures have been increasingly automated and computerized.

Then there is the whole economics and research area. This includes well educated people who forecast the direction of the economy. There are the experts analyzing interest rates. There are the planners answering questions as to those investment areas into which the firm should be going next. There are then individuals who become thoroughly expert in observing specialized industries. There are portfolio strategists who supervise strategies for major clients and their own firms.

New hires in these categories have an obvious need for considerable education. M.B.A. or other advanced degrees, including the Ph.D., are common calling cards. The principal area where the B.A. can be sufficient educational background is in direct sales activity, institutional or retail, usually the latter.

Though the careers can be both financially rewarding and intellectually stimulating, university graduates cannot count too heavily for jobs in this small area. The mergers of many firms and the phasing out of many others, due to inability to live on so-called "negotiated" commissions under new S.E.C. rules, have made the pickings slim. Nonetheless, investment banking has high allure for sophisticated graduates who have taken the time to investigate and understand a complicated and secretive field calling for high initiative and offering great individuality.

Of late, investment banking firms have been joining various commodities trading firms in taking positions for themselves or their clients in trading precious metals, meats, foreign currency, and any other kinds of commodities where fluctuating values render trading potentially profitable. The various boards of trade and firms which work in these areas offer entry-level jobs for a limited number of collegians. This is one of those areas where an agricultural background, or at least an understanding of agricultural products, can stand the young person in good stead.

One has to go directly to the firms in question for information on such non-standard careers.

CHAPTER 23

PRODUCTION MANAGEMENT, A CHIP OFF THE LEADERSHIP BLOCK

TOM MARKS is a big, friendly, highly intelligent man who wears short-sleeved shirts all year round and keeps his tie and collar perpetually loosened. He is executive vice-president and chief operating officer of a fair-sized steel manufacturing company.

"I'm basically a production man," he boomed. "I grew up on hot steel mill floors. Steel production men are tough, but they're not all John Henry, by any means. Take a look at this file."

The file he presented was a training report on a young woman, a mechanical engineering graduate. It read:

> Jane has been assigned to the supervisory force charged with start-up operations. She is currently working trims (shifts) as a supervisor in this unit. She has continued to do a good job as a startup foreman. She is gaining valuable experience with the problems associated with die life and lubrication as well as directing the hourly rated forces. She is a digger and is least happy when things are running well.

"Jane is a natural born leader, they tell me. Rides herd on 30 men, many of them twice her age, who have been working in the mill for years," Mr. Marks said. "And notice she has no fancy title, manager of this and that, or supervisor, or foreperson. She's a foreman," a title which turns some college grads off, but shouldn't. Being a foreman is a good job, one to be proud of—like being a sergeant in the U.S. Marines.

"Takes most good workers up from the ranks some 10 or 20 years to make foreman and we get some of our best ones that way. But we also like to get some strong people in like Jane, right out of college. It's the best place for a college grad to start who wants to run something someday. Like be chief executive or chief operational officer of a manufacturing company."

The line production job, the foreman's job as a starting point, is probably the most direct place for a college graduate to begin work. But production-related jobs are, of course, not all of direct foreman type, Mr. Marks explained. He pulled out several staff production or engineering progress reports. One read:

> Mr. Chivas is responsible for order and control of the inventory of all tooling (machinery) used in the Axle Division. He tests and evaluates new types and grades of tooling to determine which are best suited for the operation.

Still another report, this time on an environmental science graduate:

> Conducted an air contaminant survey to evaluate employee exposures to free silica and total dust in the hot strip mill slab yard.
> Assisted in noise survey to determine employee exposure to noise levels in the plate mill slab yard.
> Investigated a clinic case regarding alleged fume inhalation during a burning operation at the rotary shearer in the plate mills.

Or an engineering design job as performed by a newly minted civil engineer:

> During this period, Henry Miller has been assigned to the sheet and tin mill. He has done many design and sketching projects, some of the more significant being the design of a strip centering device for a welding machine on the continuous anneal line, the design of a thrust bearing cartridge for the tandem mill back-up roll bearings, and the mounting brackets for the duo mill entry reflector roll.

According to Vice-President Marks, there is no way to draw a line which separates production management work, staff or line, from "pure" engineering of a design type or at a chemical laboratory bench. What matters most to the management-oriented person is that the work offers opportunities to go on into management as opposed to purely technical activity.

Another type of staff production job he discussed seems scarcely distinguishable from computer management:

> Mrs. Novak assists with engineering technical problems that require mathematical analysis and/or development of computer programs. She has begun to become familiar with the machine language programming for the Nova mini-computer that directs the plasma arc flame cutting machine.

THE MANAGERS

One young man, an economics major with no technical background, put it eloquently in a tape interview:

"Production management is to me the essence of 'manufacturing,' which, if you look at the word, means 'making by hand.' We use brains more and machines more as substitutes for hands, but I get the same primordial feel out of it. I am making something, building something tangible. I get that direct participative sense out of it. I am close to the work and I see it rather than just think about it. I grew up on a farm and this has some of the same direct feel to it."

CHAPTER 24

MATHEMATICS, COMPUTERS, AND SYSTEMS

ANTHROPOLOGIST Margaret Mead puts forward in several different forms her thesis that, for the first time in history, the young really know more than their elders. Nowhere is this so true as in those areas of business centered on mathematics, computers, and the applications of these tools and languages to business systems. The kinds of jobs represented in the whole mix are generally those that go to people with substantial amounts of mathematics. They usually, but not always, have advanced degrees in mathematics, computer science, or operations research.

People engaged as operations research analysts apply the mathematical techniques and the computer to a wide range of technical and financial problems without limitations as to functions; that is, they may be engaged in production, finance, supply planning and other logistical activities.

Part and parcel of the operations research approach is the use of mathematical and computer models that simulate actual operating conditions. Simulation and linear programming models and various other operations research techniques are used in solving problems. It is hard to describe these to people who are not sophisticated in the area and, for those who are not, a postponement of job understanding until considerable course work has been undertaken is obviously necessary.

To give a feel for some of these projects on which the so-called "O.R." people work, operations research is used a great deal in the energy field, where the large petroleum companies construct models to help plan for effective operation of tanker fleets and crude oil tankage construction. Typically thrown into such considerations are long-range planning with such strategic variables as plans for refineries, terminating facilities, and crude oil products anticipated in the future.

Such analysts also formulate program models to assist forecasters in predicting sales volumes of product lines in geographical areas. They likewise turn their attention to the development and maintenance of corporate financial models to assist in predicting the effects of various investment strategies.

Hand in hand with the operations research people will work the computer systems analysts who are applying systems technology to a wide range of problems. These efforts are devoted to the development of effective commercial management information systems to identify systems development opportunities. The object is to develop computer tools to enable the companies and institutions in question to speed the preparation of consolidated financial statements at the end of each year, to develop real time control systems to be used by organizations dealing with extensive materials, and to incorporate employee accounting systems into integrated information systems.

Operations analysts are people who are generally applying a mix of engineering, mathematics, systems technology, and business training to provide organizations with computer tools for processing analysis and engineering design and operation. Much of this kind of activity is applied to optimize the scheduling of plant operation.

Systems analysis is applied to the controllership function, assisting management at various levels in receiving intelligence that is related to the financial and cost performance of various segments of the organization. Here, systems analysts related to other kinds of analysts and researchers will be applying their tools largely to financial decisions of the company.

A good part of general systems analysis is involved with the design and implementation of computer-oriented systems to provide business information at minimum cost and to offer management services, operations research, and other quantitative systems as needed. Here the thrust is investigating and recommending approaches to utilization of mathematical and statistical techniques in forecast and earnings preparation and analysis. The aim is to participate in the study and implementation of computer applications to finance, certainly, but also to production and marketing.

In the latter category, the organization can computerize the marketing margins statements to measure the profitability of companies and product lines, both domestic and overseas. Such workers are involved in trying to improve methods of obtaining financial data from world-wide affiliates, designing business simulators for monthly earnings, and automatically preparing financial statements from general accounting data.

CHAPTER 25

COMPUTER ARTISTS AND SCIENTISTS

ONE OFTEN HEARS about the creativity of computer and systems people. This is referring to the fact that they spend quite a bit of their time not only working on assigned problems, but in applied research that may or may not eventually result in a practical program. They are constantly experimenting.

Computer professionals have their own dreams and their own methods of expressing them through their machines. Some of their activity, in addition to being management science, has its artistic side, particularly in the development of the "software" packages that are applied. "Software" refers to the program as opposed to the machines themselves.

Computer science analysts are involved with installation and maintenance of operating systems, programming languages, programming standards, programmer training, and general purpose software packages. In a good many organizations, they are also responsible for maintaining an extensive program library of application packages in the areas of management science, engineering design, operations research, information retrieval, and financial analysis.

Literal armies of systems support and program support analysts are engaged in generating the operating systems software needed to run computer programs. They can also use sophisticated software measuring tools to optimize the use of the total computer resources. These practitioners, dealing in such computer languages as Cobol and Fortran, offer technical consulting techniques within organizations to help them make the best use of total computing resources. They help guard against computer equipment malfunction.

Certain commentators will point to the limitations of working in the areas concerned in that they are staff-oriented jobs. The contention is that once people get too deeply enmeshed in staff work, they are "over in a corner," so to speak, and unable to get into the line of more direct operating acitivites.

Such comments are becoming less and less true, because in many organizations, some of the top managers come out of computing, management science, mathematics, and operations research backgrounds. In commercial banks, for example, at least one of the top officers will have come up through the "operations" side which embraces strongly the use of math and computers and management science in the day to day work of keeping the bank going. There are quite a few corporations where the chief executives have a background in "cybernetic technology," involving computers and various mathematical techniques associated with them. There will undoubtedly be more of these, because, as one top business executive put it, "Today we swim, like it or not, in a cybernetic sea, and people must have some knowledge of the field or they will drown."

Another top executive said in highly mixed metaphors, "I have young people with me to help me because I am comparatively blind. I come of a generation that knew very little of math and computers and I have been afraid to learn much more. So, in order to keep from being totally 'snowed' by our computer jockeys, we arm ourselves with young people who serve as 'seeing eye dogs' to the blind top executives." Such young specialists become confidantes to the people at the top and naturally are in a position to be exposed to important decision-makers.

More and more of the top executives of the future probably will come out of the ranks of the technically trained. This, of necessity, means good, staunch education, even advanced training. Nonetheless, there are many opportunities for beginners in the field without technical backgrounds. Jobs as computer programmers are often open to people who have had little math and no computer science in undergraduate school. They are gradually converted into computer conversants, picking up, either on the job or in extracurricular educational activities, some further knowledge of the craft that they are going to follow. Some kind of continuous educational thrust is needed if people are going to go beyond a certain level in the computer derbies.

There are a host of jobs that cluster around the computers. A standard entry-level job for college graduates is that of programmer. A programmer converts symbolic statements of administrative data or business problems into detailed logic flow charts for coding in computer language. Such a person will analyze work flow charts or diagrams representing business problems by applying his or her knowledge of computer capabilities, subject matter, algebra, and symbolic logic in developing a sequence of program steps.

Some experience as a programmer will point to being "lead" or higher programmers and thence to posts as EDP managers. College graduates usually aspire to become managers of data processing departments or at least directors of major projects in data processing. The data processing manager is a line manager who plans, directs, and reviews business electronic data processing projects, coordinates planning, testing, and operating phases to complete the project with maximum balance of planning and equipment time. Whereas the EDP manager may have responsibility for hundreds of people in a large establishment, project managers are probably going to head a team of considerably smaller proportions and will vary the teams on which they serve according to the exigencies of the material before them.

A whole new craft has grown up around the people who sell data processing equipment or market data processing services. There are jobs with the manufacturers of computer equipment to market such equipment either on a rental or on a sales basis. This is a sales job at a high level, really a consultant, because such persons are talking in terms of whole systems and their applications, rather than just the machinery.

A complementary job is held by the technical representative who is somewhat more engineering oriented in focus than the marketing representative, but works with the marketing representative in tandem to sell and service the equipment installed.

These jobs call for college degrees and usually for an M.B.A. or some specialized management science degree.

A large number of data processing services of varying sizes have sprung up around the country. These establishments are selling the use of their machines and talent in carrying out data processing services for organizations which are either too small or too unsophisticated to carry on such activity for themselves. Clearly the use of such services can make economic and physical sense. Many college graduates are occupied in rendering service through such firms.

One of the "buzz" words in graduate business schools is "planning." The job of a planner is so broad as to almost defy description and one can't point to any single job category that fits it. It is allied with the whole computer and mathematical areas. People planning the future of companies will often use some sort of simulation model, frequently of a mathematical type. Planning usually involves financial planning, but it goes beyond that. It often can include planning for production and marketing and other functions in a business. Hence, it is cross-functional.

Comparatively few graduates of any school, graduate or undergraduate, go directly into planning. Generally it is reserved for people with a bit of experience, particularly in areas such as financial analysis. The one exception may be the comparatively few companies that take graduates out of M.B.A. schools into positions as planners for work that is a species of internal consulting. These people will work on a variety of assignments in their early stages, involving the functional area of a company.

One such new planner worked for three months on the description of the future of the market for a particular kind of machinery, worked for another three months as a member of an internal audit team, and then was thrown on a job of helping to plan the future compensation pattern to be applied to salespeople. After a year or two in such a job, these "front-end planners" will probably find themselves in other functional areas, into which they will be integrated after this initial planning period. Obviously this kind of work is very closely associated with internal consulting and, in a sense, is part and parcel of the experimental end of a general management training program.

Jobs called "planning" are frequently not career jobs, but are jobs offered to people who are going to be at it for a while and who will eventually go into something else. However, there are companies with some senior planners, directors of planning and vice-presidents of planning who are making a career out of this set of crafts. These tend to be exceptions, and planning is, by and large, a pass-through kind of experience into which people go on the way upward.

CHAPTER 26

CONSULTING—PROFESSION FOR THE EXPERIENCED

WHILE MANAGEMENT CONSULTING absorbs a fair number of university graduates a year, such careers are principally open to those with some previous experience, a bit of age on their bones, and an advanced degree, usually an M.B.A. However, this highly professional field is worth knowing something about for undergraduates too, for it may well be a calling that they will enter later.

Management consultants come in a variety of forms, from those who specialize in offering advice in a limited field to those general consultants who will provide advice in virtually any and all fields.

Unlike the public accounting profession, where passing an examination is necessary to set up one's own shingle, there are no set requirements for entry into consulting. The field has been the temporary resting place of certain jobless executives, the source of side money for professors, and a set of occupations to which retired managers can turn their hands and trade upon their accumulated wisdom.

Engineering consultants constitute one species with whom young engineers begin their careers. These are particularly active in the civil and architectural fields and are employed by companies and other institutions to help them locate and build plants and install equipment around the world, with particularly heavy emphasis on overseas activity where engineering talent is short.

There is a set of consultants that operate in the personnel and employee benefit area. They have been particularly strong in actuarial (mathematical) considerations associated with pension plans.

There are consultants in the marketing field, some specializing in industrial marketing, some in direct mail and other direct marketing, and a good many in consumer market research.

Banks, investment banks, and investment advisory firms supply considerable consultation to investors, advising their clients on where and how to invest their funds and how to apply advanced financial theory to problems.

There are other firms, some quite large, which are really computer systems specialists. Some of the accounting firms will counsel on associated problems in all the functional fields.

Then there are those consulting firms which are devoted to serving such areas as the health and hospital care fields and government at all levels.

The largest consultants can be called general management advisors. They do have specialists aboard and can work at some of the above areas, but fundamentally their work is broad, or "across the board," in scope.

The largest of the general management consultants feature at the "top of their line" advice on policy making and strategy to company executives and boards on a high level. This can be advice on organization, planning and development, and such essential functions as production and marketing. They provide an examination of arrangements at the top, including corporate planning and long-range planning for the corporation.

General management consultants, along with investment banks, commercial banks, and investment advisory firms, deal likewise in the mergers and acquisition area, helping companies acquire others or divest themselves of other companies, a complex net of planning and implementation. Financial planning in general can be involved. Consultants, particularly those with a technical bent, are strong on materials management advice in the area of inventory management and production control, warehousing, and transportation control.

General management consultants are deeply involved too with marketing, sales, and attendant problems.

Consultants are clusters of experts who exist for two major reasons:

1. The clients have problems for which they do not have the requisite internal expertise. Many such difficulties are soluble in the short term and the client does not wish to commit to hiring such expertise on a long-term basis.

2. The consultant provides a detached, objective, outside view of the firm that is more reliable in perspective than an inside view would be, where the forest may be obscured by the trees. Oddly enough, the expertise provided is often that of the external generalist, but being an informed generalist is a rare specialty.

CHAPTER 27 ━━━

INTERVIEW WITH TWO CONSULTANTS

Question. What do you like about management consulting?

Answer 1. In many ways it is a continuation of school. We are seldom on a specific engagement for more than three months, then we go on to another one. It is like a new quarter or semester, new people, fresh problems and challenges. I thrive on the variety.

Answer 2. Seldom a dull moment, though sometimes you wish the devil there were. The work is demanding, lots of time pressures, deadlines to meet, seldom quite enough time to feel you're doing a complete job.

Q. Is it specialized work? That is, do you tend to get working exclusively on personnel, or finance, or marketing assignments?

A 2. No, not really. In our firm and some of the other better ones, they take pains to switch you around from one type of assignment to the next. In my first year, for example, I worked on an organization study to restructure the executive staff of a newly merged company. This lasted for two months. Next job was to investigate the market for a new product for a farm equipment manufacturer. This took a month. Next, I traveled to northern Quebec to help develop a mine. I was away for two months on what was quite literally a community development project. I then joined a team to help devise some new operating procedures for the treasury department of a small conglomerate. So, in a short space of time, I worked with personnel, marketing, community development, and finance.

Q. Were you with different teams each time?

A 2. Quite different. I was never with any of the same folks twice. Just as they try to mix you into a variety of types of assignments, they try also to expose you to different senior consultants as your team directors and teammates. The object is to open you up to a variety of personal work styles and approaches.

Q. So you have a variety of different bosses?

A 1. Boss is not the word for it. We have senior colleagues, not bosses.

Q. Isn't it all the same?

A 1. By no means. Consulting is rather like academia. A full professor or even a department chairman is not the boss of an assistant professor. He is merely a senior colleague. The boss and peon relationship isn't there.

A 2. What Mike says is true. You've got a flat sort of organization. Some very senior colleagues are called partners or officers at a managerial level and perhaps one or two consultant ranks, senior and junior, exist, but there's little of that quasi-military hierarchy you find in so many businesses.

Q. Okay, you work with colleagues. How many of you go onto a job together?

A 1. Well, that depends on the ambitiousness of the job, of course, but three or four is the usual rule. You will have a partner in charge, a senior consultant managing the job and one or two juniors, maybe someone like us, very close to beginners. Naturally, we juniors are thrown onto the more tedious aspects, the "grunt work," and the more senior colleagues deal with the clients at the higher level.

A 2. Still, even the new people are dealing with the clients. That's why consulting firms like people with some experience, people who look and act mature. To coin a phrase, you can't send a boy to do a man's job.

Q. Are clients hard to deal with?

A 1. At the middle and lower levels they can be the toughest. Remember, it is the ones at the upper levels who ordered the study, so naturally they're cooperative. But very often the people in the departments you're studying are threatened. They see you as an investigator, an inspector, an inquisitor, possibly even a management spy. You need their cooperation desperately to get at the facts, but you have to treat them gently.

A 2. It's like anything else in business anywhere. Most of the time you're working with people over whom you have little command or control. So you have to earn their confidence if you can and gradually win them around to working with you and for you.

Q. Couldn't that be described as the essence of management?

A 1. Exactly. That's what it's all about, in consulting or in anything else.

Q. But skill with this sort of thing is hard to evaluate. How do they evaluate the performance of the individual consultant?

A 2. At the end of every engagement, any consulting firm hands in a report and set of recommendations for action. A junior consultant's colleagues are called in to evaluate the junior's contribution to the whole team project. The seniors help you along like a teacher and finally come up with a grade.

Q. A grade, quite literally?

A 1. In our firm, it's usually less arbitrary than a grade in school. At the end of any assignment, you are called in by the partner in charge, and your contribution is discussed. They tell you where you did well and also where you goofed and where you need some beefing up. It's actually pretty fair, because you get a chance to defend yourself—not to whine and deliver lame excuses, but to afford the other people some further insight into your reactions. Usually sitting in on this evaluation is the functionary who assigns consultants to further jobs. He'll thus be able to see what it is you need strengthening in.

Q. Do you ever have a hand in picking your own assignments?

A 1. Once in while. At least you can suggest what it is you might like next to the assignment officer. He exists in order to protect you from exploitation by the partners.

Q. What do you mean by exploitation?

A 1. One or several partners hopefully will take a shine to you and ask that you be assigned to work with them again and again. That's fine, except it may specialize you too much and keep you from getting the breadth of exposure you should have.

A 2. That's better than the other extreme, however. If no partners or managers are taken with you, nobody will want you on the job and that means the same as dead in our league.

Q. Sounds the same as public accounting. Is it like accounting in that its partners are the salespeople?

A 1. Yes, but for God's sake, don't ever call it sales. It's "new business." We're all very professional, you know. Like accountants, or doctors, or lawyers, we never advertise and seldom admit we sell.

A 2. The way one becomes a partner or equivalent officer in a consulting firm is to do good work and to convince the powers that be that one is the type of person who can work with clients, attract new business, be a relatively smooth and effective presenter and salesperson.

Q. On that score, I have often heard that consulting firms look for glamor boys.

A 1. And girls, these days. Well, they like attractive people. They like bright people. They tend to go for men and women at the top of their classes in top business schools.

Q. And do they succeed?

A 1. Well, much of the time. The lifestyle thing can get in the way—too much travel, too much detailed staff work drives some talent away.

A 2. But a big part of their draw is the fact that consulting is alleged to lead to good opportunities on the client side, with the corporations, for example.

Q. You say "alleged." Isn't this true?

A 2. Yeah, it's partly true, but it doesn't happen as easily as one thinks. You have to work at it. I haven't yet begun. So far in my year before the mast, nobody has winked an eye at me. But basically I'm sure we would both agree that consulting is a high class species of work that exposes one to interesting problems and people.

A 1. And pretty darn professional. You tend to learn to get to the heart of a problem and to present it well.

Q. In both writing and speaking?

A 2. Both. Your seniors will help you improve your writing by correcting your drafts over and over again, if you need it.

Q. Sounds again like school.

A 1. Yeah, but more the way school ought to be than it is.

CHAPTER 28

INS AND OUTS OF GOVERNMENT JOBS

As THE UNITED STATES has become more populous and more involved in providing public services, the number of jobs offered at varied levels of government has increased. The better ones go to college graduates.

In most respects these jobs are not different in kind from private business jobs, except that one is dealing with public business rather than private. There are accountants, budget analysts, digital computer programmers, management analysts and interns, personnel managers and marketing (public relations) specialists, and then a variety of chemists, dieticians, entomologists, mathematicians, veterinarians, and other non-business categories.

Many of the administrative jobs with government require a basic college degree. For some of the specialized jobs and for entry at higher levels, advanced training in a specialty or in business administration or public administration can be indicated.

Government is one of the major employment systems in the country, employing a whopping 17 million persons in federal agencies, state governments, counties, cities, and municipalities. Actually it would surprise many to learn that the federal government comprises the smallest (2.8 million) unit compared to state employees (4 million) and county and municipal employees (8 million).

It is the smaller federal sector that receives the most recognition when one thinks of working for the government. Perhaps this is fortunate because certainly it is the best organized sector, the easiest for the talented student to approach, and it offers on the whole a career ladder the most free from the hot and cold blowings of the political winds. Yet there are some good jobs in each of the sectors for those willing to seek them out.

"Seek them out" is a major clue to success in the civil service realms. Compared with private companies, the agencies of all the governments do little organized college recruiting. They do send representatives around to speak to students, but often they do not interview them as individuals, since interviews are not a principal criterion of hiring. The student must of necessity take the positive steps to register for and complete the frequently lengthy procedure of taking examinations and waiting for the results. Finally, if a job opens up and one has scored near the top of the list on the exam, one gets a job. Some states and municipalities also follow the examination procedures and have their own version of civil service.

Most entry-level jobs for collegians in the federal sector will be obtained through taking the Professional and Administrative Career Examination known as P.A.C.E. It is a standardized test for inexperienced college graduates with non-technical degrees. Covering the verbal, mathematical, and judgmental ability areas, the scores on individual applicants are referred to the various agencies listing vacancies.

The federal job market frequently is tight and the number of candidates large. In these years only a small percentage of those qualifying actually get jobs.

Some occupations require a technical degree or specialized background and are filled by individual numbered announcements. Applicants need not take the P.A.C.E. examination, but are evaluated on the basis of education and experience.

College graduates typically qualify for the GS-5 and GS-7 levels. Further details can be obtained by students from the U.S. Civil Service Commission officer in the major cities of the country.

Certain federal agencies have their own systems outside the Civil Service competitive system and a number of quasi-governmental agencies also are not part of the system. This is not to mention the countless non-federal jobs which need to be tracked in every state and local nook and cranny.

People holding M.B.A. or M.P.A., J.D., Ph.D. and other advanced degrees may also qualify for mid-level jobs at the GS-9 through the GS-12 levels. These jobs are based on education and experience without a test. There has been comparatively little such hiring going on in recent years, yet one may reason that government will continue to burgeon and, with it, so will the jobs.

Since profit is not the motive, government employment can create a different feel for employees than a job in private business. There are those who like this aspect and those who do not. One has to judge in which sector one would be the most comfortable. It is often said that the resultant efficiencies in the private sector are superior, but inefficiency is to be found anywhere. Efficiency in a budgeting sense substitutes for profit as an incentive in the public sector. One has to decide about the effects of personal and organizational competition in the two sectors.

CHAPTER 29

BRIEF ENCOUNTER WITH A CIVIL SERVANT

Question. What is it you do with the state government, Moira?

Answer. I work as special assistant to the state insurance commissioner. That means generally that I do a variety of special jobs for him, but I'm not his "girl Friday." This is not a glorified secretarial job, but an administrative post and a pretty fair one.

Q. Is it covered by the state civil service act?

A. No. As far as I'm concerned, civil service offers fairly plodding jobs that move you up the clerical ladder. Oh, eventually you do become superclerk, but that's not for me.

Q. Did you ever apply for a federal job?

A. Yes, and I got on the P.A.C.E. examination list with a score in the mid-90s, which is fairly high. I'm still on the list, but I wouldn't take the job if it came through. It pays less than I'm getting and I think I'm having more fun being the bigger frog in the smaller pond. My boss is a good guy who wants me to learn. He's up there, you know, a member of the governor's cabinet. He's still comparatively young and may run for governor himself some day. Maybe I'll be in the numbers when the saints come marching in. I just don't really have the patience to go through the slow civil service dance.

Q. But you like the idea of government work?

A. Oh, sure. I've kind of got a theory about it. I feel, well, sort of patriotic. Like I'm really doing something for my state or my country, I guess. Lots of young people feel that way and a lot more did until recently, but there just haven't been enough jobs, and people have to eat. Many of us were inspired by Ralph Nader and the Legal Aid Society and all that sort of thing. But it turned out there isn't room for more than one Ralph Nader and the jobs are few.

Q. Had you thought of law as appropriate schooling?

A. Yes, as a matter of fact, but I get back to that wanting to eat business. And I wanted to show the folks that I could hold a job after living off them for so long. So far, I've just settled for a political science degree, but I might start law at night, who knows? Insurance involves a lot of legal questions and my boss, the commissioner, is an attorney.

Q. If the governor loses the election or your boss gets sacked, aren't you out of a job?

A. Probably. But it's good experience, and I'll bounce on to something else on the government side. The way I see it, the best jobs and the top jobs in government service are appointive—that is, you come in at a pretty good level as someone appointed by someone else. Of course, you have to get started somewhere, and I can understand kids trying to start near the bottom with some of the big stable shows such as the Postal Service, HEW, Treasury, and the like. Depends on your temperament, I guess. But to get started with these outfits, you've got to be willing to start lower than you really should, go anywhere they want you to go. I'd rather be more selective.

Q. How did you get your job?

A. Quite frankly, my boss's daughter and I graduated together from college and I met him at graduation. My parents and her parents hit it off well at that time and my boss finally got around to asking me my plans. He had just become commissioner and he really liked my social service pitch. Lucky day it was.

CHAPTER 30

THE SMALL BUSINESS TRAINEE

No MATTER HOW BLEAK the outlook may at times seem for the college graduate seeking jobs, there are always thousands of jobs unfilled. That is an irony compounded by the fact that thousands of smaller businesses have no tradition of coming to college campuses to recruit. Actually, they have unwarranted inferiority complexes about competing with large employers for talent. They are unfamiliar with recruitment and hence afraid they have too little to offer when they just have a job or two open for college graduates. Actually, one job is all anybody wants and hundreds of students would be delighted at the challenges of small business.

All this is complicated by the fact that students too are as frightened and non-adventurous as the smaller employers. If the students are willing to explore or canvass by mail or in person the hundreds of smaller businesses in the functional or geographic area of their interests, they would be bound to come across some opportunities.

All but the tiniest "Mom and Pop" enterprise run by the immediate family has need for new blood, new young people—unless the enterprise is a failing one. Many smaller proprietors cannot wait for sons or daughters to grow up; many have no such people, either capable or interested, waiting in the wings.

Here an odd mixture of daring and humility serves the young person well. On the daring side lies the proposal to the smaller business proprietor that he take on a young college graduate. Surprisingly enough, the answer sometimes is, "Well, you know, we've been thinking about that, but we've never quite known how to go about it. We're always afraid that young people these days will want too much and want to work too little."

The answer to that objection is, "I want to learn the business from somebody good like you, that's what I want, and I'm willing to pay the price for this learning, though I want a chance not only to learn it, but to some day own a corner of it. I'm willing to do what you suggest."

Of course, collegians have no intention of working for nothing and must help set the wages and the prospects. They can get insights on the wages from their college placement director, and they must satisfy themselves on the prospects or by quizzing their future bosses persistently.

It is a fact of work life that one must be ready to meet one's bosses half way in guiding and designing a career. Few bosses, current or prospective, are mind readers and need to be fed some of their lines by the intelligent people they hire. Most bosses are too preoccupied with running their shows to be as alert as they should be to the needs of each of their subordinates. The smaller the business the more this is true, and the less likely the company is to have its own articulated recruiting and management development procedures.

In the final analysis, there may be no better way for a graduate from a bachelor's-degree program to get a start than through a general training program, formal or informal. This is not starting from the bottom in the sense a high school graduate would, but there is a necessity for the kind of perspective that starting from the bottom demands.

CHAPTER 31

CALLING ON SMOKESTACKS, OR SMOKING OUT A JOB

As ARE THE OTHER ILLUSTRATIONS in this book, this is an account of a situation which actually took place not too long ago.

Phil Henderson was a young Chicagoan who lived on the West Side. Every day for four years of undergraduate business schooling, Phil drove down Pulaski Avenue to his university and to work on a part-time job. Pulaski is a street of many smokestacks on many factories of modest size. As he drove, Phil often wondered what was going on behind the plant walls.

As his graduation approached, Phil expressed this wonderment to his favorite marketing professor. "Well, why don't you devote some time to finding out, if you're really interested," his professor advised. "Maybe it'll lead to that small business job you say you'd like. Salespeople make cold calls on smokestacks and smoke out new customers that way. Of course, they try to find out what they can about the organizations first."

So Phil "cased" some of the companies. Most were too small to be listed in the usual business directories or to issue annual reports. He checked the phone book, the roster of the Chicago Association of Commerce and Industry, and some of his father's friends. His father was a tool and die maker familiar with some of the machine shops and smaller factories in the area.

He narrowed his targets to 10 plants working in product areas that interested him. At each plant, he would walk in the front door and ask to see the chief executive. When the secretary asked for his name and business, he would indentify himself as a marketing student at a business school, doing a project on the uses of modern marketing techniques by smaller businesses. This was indeed true, but it was not the main purpose of his proposed visit, which was, instead, to investigate job possibilities.

With the exception of one witch at the switch, the receptionists

100

were polite and helpful. Two switched him to sales managers and he interviewed them. At three more companies, he actually got in to see the top executive. Each seemed to be flattered that someone from the university bothered to call on them. They also displayed some curiosity as to what was being taught in undergraduate business schools. One of them had not really known what the term "marketing" meant and how it differed from sales. He turned out to be the most interesting of the lot.

His name was August Spink, and he was chairman, president, and principal owner of a firm which manufactured dental supplies. Phil explained to him the concepts of modern marketing as he had learned them at school. Mr. Spink proved unfamiliar with these ideas, but had a lively curiosity about them. To him, marketing spelled sales, nothing more and nothing less, and his only marketing employee was a sales manager. The older man kept Phil talking for a full three hours, but Phil didn't mind. They bandied ideas; they argued pleasantly.

Finally, Phil rose to leave and Mr. Spink said, "I tell you what, if you're game, I'd like you to come over here two weeks from Saturday to talk with my directors and some of my other people. I'd like you to prepare a little spiel on what marketing is and can be. And I'll pay you $100 for the morning. How does that strike you?"

Needless to say, it struck Phil very well. His talk before the directors led to an assignment to do a small market research project for the company. To his surprise, Phil discovered that these people did not even know how many dentists comprised their market. It was quite easy to dazzle them with a few simple facts picked up from a few easily available sources.

It was a bit less of a surprise some two months later when Mr. Spink, with whom he had really gotten on famously, broached the subject of a permanent job. Phil took it.

Two years later, Phil held the post of director of marketing for this $12,000,000 a year company. He had served his stint in sales, as an assistant in the plant, and as direct assistant to August Spink. August has no successors at 60 years of age. Phil is probably a safe bet to be treated "like a son."

CHAPTER 32

WORK IS WHERE YOU MAKE IT

IT'S UNLIKELY that a very high proportion of human beings are doing completely what they want to do and making a living at it. Still there are those who are, and it's foolish for promising people to abandon the goal without trying to come as close to it as possible.

Take the case of two young men. Both are Europeans. Both are making careers for themselves connected with recreation.

The first, a young Frenchman, is a graduate of an undergraduate liberal arts program in a large American university. He went back to Paris upon graduation and spent time as a newspaper reporter, a career with which he got bored rather quickly. Perhaps it's more accurate to say that he was bored with the city life and longed for some chance to breathe fresh air and to flex his muscles a bit.

His most pleasant assignment was to cover an interesting business story. A young Englishman had purchased an old river barge in France and converted it from a coal carrier to a small floating hotel. He then promoted one-week tourist trips down various rivers and canals in central France. He served good food and wines, provided bicycles and small boats for recreation and sailed his barge at a slow pace where he chose. The barge tied up every night and its passengers were encouraged to explore, with some guidance, the towns and the countryside en route.

This approach to the tourist trade was at once novel and quite successful. Tourists, principally British and American, took very quickly to a novel alternative to the automobile, bus, or railroad. The barge appealed to them as a leisurely alternative, which gave them the real feel of the countryside.

The young French reporter signed on with the British owner as a deckhand and made his way successively up to partner, investing some money and earnings in ownership. He now combines recreational management with his own sports—swimming, boating, hiking,

102

biking, and lovemaking—with making a fair living. As one who had traveled on his boat put it, "We all had great fun, but I believe the members of the crew enjoyed it even more than we did."

Across the channel on the western seacoast of highland Scotland, another young collegian, a Welsh marine engineering graduate, has done something similar. He borrowed money and with it purchased a 75-foot wooden fishing trawler some 50 years of age to carry fishing parties out of a picturesque holiday village onto one of the deep sea lochs, or bays. He is gradually refitting the vessel for recreational service with the proceeds and paying himself a competency.

The sea and fixing up old boats had long been his hobbies and now they are his occupation. He professes to be as happy as a clam.

Of course, complete recreational happiness is not necessarily everyone's aim out of a work life. Probably the majority of people are quite willing to sacrifice some of their hedonistic goals for money, status, power, sense of achievement. None of these goals is holy, inviolate, or necessarily prescribed for all. Sometimes it is hard to tell before experience at working where one puts one's values and goals.

While it is wise psychology to pick the first job with care, especially if there is a choice, it is also wise to realize that the first job is not necessarily the last. One can always change one's mind and usually, eventually, find a more suitable role—if the individual can determine what the role will be.

Many moderns are much taken up with the matter of "lifestyle," which can be interpreted as a matter of how one lives and where, as much as what the work will be. Such a preoccupation is a rightful one for those whose lives are heavily focused on such values.

Strong geographical preferences—country over city, one section of the country before all others—these are important factors to feed into job search and choice.

Frequently a person with a rather rare or commercially remote set of preferences will have to go "on foot" to the area in question, make inquiry of all available job information sources in the area and then call on these choices in person or by mail, followed up with visits. You cannot necessarily wait for appropriate smaller companies to come on your campus to hire. None may come, so the battle must be carried to the employers.

Jobs in small business are there. It is, of course, difficult for a young person to find the capital to start such an enterprise. Some knowledge of a field is necessary. That's why so many graduates learn their trade at somebody's expense. Those who embark on small business careers do well to remember that such firms tend to founder on two counts. The first is a lack of knowledge as to how to promote the business to the market served and the second is a failure to be able to make the requisite decisions decisively. Such abilities are not often present early in life.

If the college graduate is not too proud to go into modest callings of comparatively low prestige, working at managing and eventually owning fast food franchises, gas stations, scavenger services, and the like, the individual's chances to succeed are good, since the competition in these areas, in terms of business acumen, is probably at lower levels than in competing fields traditionally drawing college graduates.

Such work requires some sacrifice of middle class pride and certainly demands a willingness to work long and hard.

Generally speaking, the satisfactions of running one's own show, of being beholden to no one, can be worth the sacrifice. One can reflect that the United States was built westward by men and women who turned their hands to whatever needed to be done. They lived in wagons or shacks or behind or above stores. Such reminders may sound like the material one hears in commencement addresses, but that doesn't really detract from the facts. Invention is not limited to machines and gadgets. Somebody invented the laundromat, the fast food chain, the do-it-yourself picture frame shop, the travel agency, the tax consulting office, the auto, truck, trailer, and tool rental firms. Such activities did not exist 50 years ago; some are very recent inventions which have provided interesting and profitable livelihoods for their inventors and pioneers.

There will be many more such innovations in the years ahead as society and technology change. Today's college graduates will be at the heart of these changes—at least those people who are inventive and creative.

It has been said that a good person never takes a job but makes a job. Such people shape any assignment to their own persons and ideas. Most jobs are malleable; they can be shaped. An enterprising person is never without something to do. If a current assignment is completed and no immediate next one is provided, the alert person can spot things to be done.

One business school student was told by his part-time employer, a necktie manufacturer, "we've run out of work for you, Alex."

"Nonsense," replied Alex. "Have you ever thought of selling the idea of trademarked company ties to companies and 'old school' ties to universities?"

No, they hadn't. When he'd finished selling hundreds of ties to dozens of institutions, Alex came up with the idea of similarly designed scarves for women. The business of the company has tripled and his own income quadrupled as a result of his refusal to run out of work.

CHAPTER 33

INTERNATIONAL IS NOT
A JUNIOR YEAR ABROAD

MANY AMERICAN STUDENTS and graduates will tell you they would like to be in what they call International Business. You question them a bit further and may find that they think international is a whole separate world for which one can prepare specifically and in which one spends a careertime. It becomes obvious too that woven into the work fantasies are pictures of dressing for dinner in the tropics, intrigue on the Orient Express, springtime in Paris, jet plane conferences with the Shah of Iran. Now there's nothing wrong with a few fantasies as long as they are recognized as such.

While it is true that business remains one of the few institutions that can still rise above the parochial pettiness of nations, international business is, in the main, an extension of domestic business, rather than some glamorous universe apart.

In an age of airplanes, much international business is carried on from American cities and those engaged in it travel out from home. They see much more of hotel and plant meeting rooms than they do of the boulevards or bistros of foreign capitals.

It is difficult, in the face of increasingly strict visa and work permit regulations, for Americans to work overseas on an expatriate basis. Ironically, those who do get such assignments have a tendency to find that such difficulties as the schooling for their families and isolation from centers of power and preference make them long for the sights and sounds of home. Also, those who are "fortunate" enough to be assigned overseas billets often do find the work little more stimulating and often more frustrating from the point of view of bureaucratic limitations than the domestic variety of managerial work.

While there are some economic, monetary, legal, procedural, and cultural problems unique to overseas activity, in the main, business is business the world over.

One can prepare for international activity by taking courses in international economics, foreign trade, political relations, languages, and cultural area studies. But, of course, the pursuit of such studies does not guarantee trans-national involvement.

There are some good exchange programs available through American universities to spend weeks, months, or a year or two in a foreign school of business or economics or politics. Some of the people who have such experience can manage to stay overseas or get into foreign relations jobs, through their contacts or their professors.

But one needs to be wary. There are plenty of grandiose-sounding international academic sequences that carry little international job power. They are no guarantees of positions and often lead to disillusionment for many, fulfillment for a very few.

Perhaps the surest way to engineer an eventual overseas berth is to start in a domestic job with an international firm, work away at learning the stateside ropes and at finding out what jobs may be coming up by listening for them on the inside. Such alertness, plus some appropriate academic and cultural background, can lead to the right personnel card being speared out of the right file drawer at the right time for the international aspirant.

Foreign students in the United States have problems getting hired in international business, though their chances are probably better than those for their American counterparts. Foreign students frequently want to work in the United States for a time, at least, and can sometimes succeed for a few months, working under the training period provisions of their U.S. visas. A larger number of them these days are having to go back home immediately.

While competence in a foreign language is obviously helpful to international careers, it is by no means a guarantee of such. The number of Americans with multilingual competency increases every year. Their competency is often abetted by travel or living abroad. The need for translators is small. English has become the standard commercial language and the majority of foreign international business people are quite capable in it.

One gets into international activity with luck, persistence, and some appropriate training, but international is not a very steady vehicle on which most can hitch a ride. For some who succeed, however, the rewards can be great. The excitement of travel, the feeling of internationality, the association with a multinational set of executives—all these elements can be stimulating. Companies with international operations have a tendency to draw their top people from those who have had overseas stints. Despite all the difficulties of gaining such posts, they may well be worth the struggle.

CHAPTER 34

SPECIAL OPPORTUNITIES AND PROBLEMS FOR OLDER STUDENTS AND GRADUATES

THE AVERAGE AGE of students in colleges and universities has been rising steadily in the last decade. The popularity of continuing education, much of it on a part-time basis, has helped insure that. The concept of career mobility has caught on too, and one finds experienced men and women returning to school full-time to engineer career changes.

There is a great variety in ages and circumstances. There is the somewhat older student still in the 20s. Such people, when they are from one to eight years older than the pattern of those who take their schooling in one piece, tend to have little trouble fitting into the entry-level jobs. In fact, they often have the advantage that some maturity brings. This is the kind of advantage that has enabled the universities and the economy to absorb the veterans of our various recent wars. Many employers and graduate schools prize these somewhat seasoned people.

Up to the threshold of 30 or so, a dash of extra age can be good in the mix. Beyond that point, age can start operating as a negative, unless it is accompanied by appropriate experience, that is, the kind of experience that counts with the employer.

Students and graduates over 30 with direct business or administrative experience can be taken on at a somewhat higher than entry-level job, allowing for that experience. But the over-30-year-old whose experience has not seemed very directly applicable—be it school teaching, higher scholarship, social work, military, Peace Corps, blue collar work, housewifery—these people often will not be courted by employers. They may have dug a career trench out of which it will be difficult to climb.

Why will employers take a dim view of such people? Well, a main barrier is asking a 32-year-old to take the same job as a 22-year-old. This makes employers uncomfortable and frequently makes the applicant uncomfortable also, particularly if he or she is the type of person who wants extra money and attention just for having lived longer. Naturally the employer's fear of having to pay more is a factor in all such negotiations.

Throwing thirtyish graduates into entry-level training programs can be hard on the graduates, who may regard the process as "kid stuff." Then too, many firms and corporations operate on development timetables that establish that by age 35, say, a person should be a partner or a manager partway up the ladder. So, if you are dealing with a person who just got going at age 34, where does that person fit in the scheme?

Many an employer hews to a theory of the relatively fast start, feeling that leadership traits and managerial ability will surface early— during the 20s. "What do we do with people who are just getting started at 30 and have not previously demonstrated any traits of leadership or supervisory promise? Maybe they have never had a chance to do so, but is that our problem?" comments an employer.

One result of awakened female consciousness has been the woman returning to school and hopefully turning to a new career after "X" number of years as a wife and often as a mother. That is all well and good, many an employer will say. "But what am I to do with a 37-year-old woman coming in as a new employee in early middle age? How can I fit her in with the youngsters? Can I train her? Well, maybe, if I have the time."

On the credit side of the ledger, there are those employers who have found that older hires, particularly women returning to the work force, make steadier workers than their younger counterparts who presumably have more to distract them and are less serious about careers. Older graduates understandably are equipped with more of a sense of urgency to make up for lost time.

Going "back to school" at higher than normal ages has a tendency to be a very career-motivated act. It can represent a thrust to change life direction, career direction, social class direction. We have already observed that college training is the strongest rite of passage for those seeking to achieve middle class professional stations.

Mature students beyond 30 will not necessarily find employers believing that an additional degree or two alone merits their being hired as a potential manager. Too often, their new intentions are simply not regarded as "believable." It makes sense for any such person with an intent to take more schooling to seek advice from placement and employment persons before plunking down chunks of time and tuition, unless schooling is motivated by considerations beyond sheer career movement.

Of course, there are all sorts of school programs. A first degree in anything may help in social class advance. Business schooling can be useful to people who have none of it. Additional degree work in one's own specialty (i.e., engineering) can be a new ticket.

But keep in mind that even those employers who pay tuition for additional schooling will not necessarily base promotion on new degrees or academic attainment. Unresearched, unchecked faith in degrees alone as career fuel can lead to frustration.

Of course, there are many examples of those "late bloomers" who have restarted life at 30, 40, even 50. Through persuasiveness, obvious talent, and sincerity, they have convinced those who hire them that they are both serious about a new start and will do a good job. That latter point is important. No company feels that it owes a living to those of any age who will not contribute to improving productivity, efficiency, and profit.

CHAPTER 35

SUMMING UP

THOSE WHO HAVE read this book up to this point will sense the inadequacy of the old refrain that those who tried other professions and failed used to sing, "Well, there's always business."

Business is not for everyone; it represents a set of professions which are demanding and selective. They require not only a good education, but a species of toughness and adaptability not possessed by all human beings.

Though not in infinite supply, happily there are a large number of premanagerial and managerial jobs open every year for the college educated. They represent a far greater number of opportunities of greater variety than those to be found in any of the other professions.

Happily too, executives and managers are well paid, not only at the top of the pyramid where they rival the recompense of those at the top in any other professions, but in a wide middle and lower range of management jobs. Entry level jobs start in at $10,000 and up, and it is not too uncommon to find graduates "making their age," that is, $30,000 at 30, $35,000 at 35, and so forth.

Managerial work can be intellectually challenging too. Graduate business curricula and job content in a complex age can rival that of any of the other professions in cerebration required.

Psychic rewards are numerous, such as the satisfactions of command and leadership, the thrill of the risk and game, the exhilaration of the sale, the sense of contribution to the company and to society. All these are open to the many people who are in business, but obviously not to every aspirant.

A management career must be nurtured and cultivated. It requires a sense of self-marketing built around such themes as "How can I do a better job? How can I gain more visibility? What should be my next move? Which decision should I make?"

Decisions (or the absence of them) are at the heart of a career. It starts with a decision on schooling, on first job, and on pathways

112

thereafter. There are more elements in the control of a decisive individual than indecisive people care to admit.

And career is process. Planning plays a part, but the results lie in execution. The live elements of an interview cannot be hypothesized in advance. Prior self-assessment has its limitations. It is only in the processes of marketing oneself, of performing work, of interacting with people that true self-perception may emerge. Post-college job placement through the actual market is a very different thing from going through a career planning course.

Undoubtedly too many younger people have been sold a bill of goods by placement personnel, professors, and schools. They have been encouraged positively, or simply through the neglect of adequate counseling, to go into work for whic'· they have little promise of success. Frequently this has been accompanied by self-delusion as well, which compounds the social and personal loss. Too many people have sought to go into administrative work in recent years by default, because so many other career avenues have appeared to be closed.

In the career process, one should be constantly alert to signs of external and internal reaction. "What does my success on this project tell me? What inference should I draw from my failure to gain the promotion I wanted?" Answers to these questions help shape a career.

One of the glories of business management lies in the great variety of jobs and tracks, so that a larger number of different types can be accommodated than in some of the traditional professions. It is important in the process to keep refreshing one's insights about one's own talents and preferences.

Some people aver, for example, that there is a distinction between the leader and the manager. A manager is a problem solver, a compromiser, a person who likes working with and through people to establish strategies and make decisions.

Far less conservative and more individualistic, so the theory goes, is the leader touched by "greatness." Leaders are characterized as imaginative, daring risk-takers. Unlike the conservator-manager, the leader's sense of identity is not submerged in the organization, but endures quite separate from it.

Whatever the accuracy of these speculations, it is certain that people with both leadership and managerial stripes are needed. The important question is where one sees oneself as standing compared to these and other archetypes. The courses and companies one chooses would ideally be picked on the basis of where one feels the most stimulated or the most comfortable, depending on whether the individual values stimulation or comfort or a blend of the two.

To the leader-manager dichotomy such management writers as Peter Drucker would introduce a third species, the knowledge worker. Though better educated and trained, the knowledge worker is characterized as a white collar version of the traditional worker, in short, neither leader nor manager, and perhaps not much of a professional.

Well, the determination of where you stand among these models will color your own view of yourself and hence your career. Very few rise to the peak. Most people have to settle for goals that are not officially the loftiest. They reach the level of their own competence (or some say incompetence) and from that point must find ways to enrich the plateau on which they stand.

Sure as shooting, you will someday be middle aged and probably you will see no further upward movement possible. You may turn to making sure that you are the best darned whatever you are in the country, whether knowledge worker or manager. You may want to enhance your education, your professional skill and stature. Perhaps "pro bono" work for the good of your community will excite you. Maybe travel, sailboating, or music will take up some of the energies previously directed to career upward mobility.

In these adaptations, you will come to appreciate your investment in education. It should afford you the perspective of the centuries, which is the ability to be detached enough from the struggle to not take your comparative successes and comparative disappointments so utterly seriously as to incapacitate you from doing your part in helping keep the world running. Such equanimity should also prevent you from boring either yourself or your companions.